SKYE

A Travellers' Guide

Christine Wiener

The Grasshopper Press

Z 013388 R

First published 1979
ISBN 0 904701 06 9

The Grasshopper Press
12 Church Street, Fenstanton, Huntingdon

Designed by Graham Taverner

Illustrations by Jack Lewis

Set in 11/12pt Theme
Printed and bound in Great Britain by
Labute Ltd.
Cambridge

CONTENTS

FERRY AT ARMADALE

KYLEAKIN

Approaches to Skye

The Isle of Skye — a rather shapeless landmass some fifty miles long and at its narrowest no more than four miles across — lies off the north-west coast of Scotland. The Outer Hebrides are more isolated; other islands in the Inner Hebrides group are further off from the mainland. Yet Skye, on the road to nowhere, seems infinitely remote.

It is a land of mist and grape-blue mountains, of deep lochs whose surface when unruffled shines like black glass, of clear streams singing over shiny pebbles, of silver sands, dancing waves and treacherous rock, of peat bogs and long stretches of tough sea-grass — the machair. Around its ruined castles and crofts, in the fishing villages and small towns, all grey stone and whitewash, the tenor of life on Skye is ageless; it seems as old as the volcanic upheaval from which the island rose.

Certainly, the present is encroaching. Skye has its light industry, which provides some much-needed employment for the islanders, and its airport, with regular services from the mainland. Tourists come and go away again; others, attracted by the property bargains the islands offer, come to settle in Skye, bringing with them the consumer goods of modern society. There is television on the island, and self-service shops. But you can still drive twenty miles and more without meeting another car and walk for hours with nothing but the Blackface sheep for company.

5

Remote then, and largely unchanged, the special charm of Skye where 'peace comes dripping slow' takes time to sink in: the day-tripper may be stunned by the scenery; only to the traveller reaching journey's end will Skye reveal its many secret faces.

Since the Norsemen first came over the seas to Skye, many travellers have taken the 'road to the Isles' and nowadays, we can follow in their steps with the added amenities of up-to-date transport. We could, for instance, do worse than retrace the road taken by Dr. Johnson.

On the 18th of August 1773, Dr. Johnson left Edinburgh and travelled up the east coast to Inverness, with his faithful Boswell, himself a Scotsman, as cicerone. From there, they rode over the high, heather-clad hills and along the shores of Loch Ness. Dr. Johnson writes: 'We took two Highlanders to run beside us, partly to shew us the way, and partly to take back from the sea-side the horses, of which they were the owners.' They arrived at Fort Augustus on the 30th and were made comfortable there by Governor Trapaud, his wife, daughter and son-in-law, all 'most obliging and polite'. It was to be their last taste of civilisation for some time to come.

The road today, cut deep into the rock and well-surfaced and maintained, runs along the northern shore of the loch, through a changing landscape of hill, woodland and water. Loch Ness itself is 24 miles long and never more than a mile across. Its depth is still debated: it is at its deepest (some 750 feet) by the ruined shell of Urquhart Castle. The castle, standing on a buff overlooking the loch, is at the head of the glen of the same name, a beautiful enclave of pasture land and magnificent copper beeches in sudden contrast to the sombre pines and pale green larches which clothe the hillside for most of the way. Along this road, an efficient coach service crosses Scotland at one of its narrowest points and links Inverness to Fort William, via Fort Augustus.

Of the Fort itself, as Johnson and Boswell knew it, there is virtually nothing left. It was built after the 1715 rebellion to subdue the Highlanders. In 1876, it was given by the Lord Lovat of the day to Benedictine monks, and today, their modern buildings incorporate all that is left of the old Fort. A church and a school also stand in the monastery's beautifully wooded grounds at the head of the lake, at its meeting point with the Caledonian Canal. Within a ten minute walk along the Canal banks, there are three pretty white-painted locks and, with any luck, a small ship will make its way slowly through the gates. The cutting of the Canal was started in 1805 under the direction of the famous Scottish civil engineer, Thomas Telford, a self-taught farm lad from Dumfriesshire. It links four lochs over a distance of about 60 miles and where it enters Loch Oich (north of Fort William), it is a hundred feet above sea level. As such, the Caledonian Canal is an early token of the ingenuity of Scottish engineering. Coming into Fort Augustus, cutting straight through the moors, it is seen at its best.

Leaving Fort Augustus, Dr. Johnson and Boswell made their way, still on horseback and duly approvisioned, through wild mountainous country down to the coast. At Glenelg, they embarked in an open boat for 'Armidel in Sky' — as they spelt it then.

Today, thousands of tourists pour into Skye each year through Armadale Pier, on the ferry service from the fishing port of Mallaig. From the pier, the road turns left to Ardvasar, which provides the nearest hotel and guest house accommodation to the landing-stage. Turning right, the road north runs through the wooded policies of Armadale Castle, the seat of Lord MacDonald of Sleat — the name given to this southernmost tip of the island, as well as to the sound, or channel, which separates it here from the mainland. The present castle was built in 1815: the original residence of the MacDonalds of Sleat having been burnt down by King William's troops after the battle of Killiecrankie in 1689. For travellers in the Armadale district, Boswell gives a tempting taste of the landscape: 'Armidale', he writes, 'is situated on a pretty bay of the narrow sea, which flows between the main land of Scotland and the Isle of Skye. In front there is a grand prospect of the rude mountains of Moidart and

Knoidart. Behind are hills gently rising and covered with finer verdure than I expected to see in this climate, and the scene is enlivened by a number of little clear brooks.' This eastern coast of Sleat, the 'garden of Skye', is in sharp contrast to the region south of Ardvasar, which is wild and barren, but well worth exploring for its beautiful views of hills, sea and islands — Eigg, Rum and Canna to the south, and the Outer Hebrides far off in the west. During the season, the car ferry from Mallaig runs at two-hourly intervals six days a week. There are other, and perhaps better, approaches to Skye, but Armadale provides a good opportunity to get to know an attractive part of the island. And for those in search of literary associations, there is the thrill of standing on the spot where, on Thursday, the 3rd of September 1773, Sir Alexander MacDonald of Sleat waited on the sands to welcome his weary guests, Dr. Johnson and James Boswell, Esquire.

We had left them setting off from the Great Glen two days earlier, on the last lap of their journey to Skye. The route they took can be roughly followed today — through Glen Shiel and, by a winding road, over the top of Ratagan Range, down to the coast at Glenelg for the crossing to Kylerhea. But this involves some very heavy driving, and a less strenuous road leads back south to Fort William.

The town lies on the shores of Loch Linnhe, at the foot of mighty Ben Nevis. Grey stone houses along the single High Street which runs parallel to the lake, ends in a neat promenade of lawns and flower beds. More grey houses on the steep hill across the way, churches of several denominations, some hotels, a war memorial — there you have the 'gateway to the Highlands', as Fort William is very properly called. In 1690 General Mackay built there a strong post in the heart of disaffected country and named it after the King (William III), but the town originated in a fort garrisoned under General Monk, during the Commonwealth, again for the purpose of overawing the Highlanders. Today there is virtually nothing left of its past. Rather it has a prim Victorian air, a little sour and forbidding at first sight. Yet, its people are friendly enough, its hotels comfortable, its shops good, and there is more in Fort William to see and do than might at first appear.

For those in search of Stuart memories, there is, for instance, the little West Highland Museum which contains the curious portrait of Bonnie Prince Charlie painted on glass as well as many other 'treasonable' relics of the times.

A selection of Highland weapons includes broadswords, bullets and the pincers used to mould them, flints, powder-horns and the multi-purpose dirk, with its long sharp blade, some of these instruments of war picked up on the field of Culloden. Illustrating more peaceful pursuits, agricultural implements of the time are hung round the walls: a flail, a winnowing-sieve made of sheep's hide and the wooden rattle which served as a scarecrow. The most vivid as well as the most charming illustration of everyday life, however, is the collection of hand-high dolls each dressed in the contemporary style and carrying the appropriate tools of the trade—a crofter with his foot-plough, the cas chrom; a plaided woman with her creel of peat, cut and dried for firing. In contrast to this simplicity there are displays of upper-class finery—embroidered silk waistcoats and a lace Shetland shawl, spun so delicately that it threads through the newly married lady's wedding ring.

But the treasure of the collection is undoubtedly the 'Secret Portrait', used by Jacobites to drink the forbidden toast to Prince Charles Edward, 'the King over the water'. A polished cylinder stands on a wooden tray smeared with an apparently meaningless blur of paint. But the cylinder itself reflects a perfect miniature of the Prince. This rare curiosity was discovered in a London junk shop; its artist is unknown.

Fort William's other wonder is, of course, Ben Nevis. 'The Ben — as it is known locally—is the highest mountain in the British Isles. There is some dispute about its actual height: 4,600ft. is commonly quoted, and that makes it some 400ft. taller than Wales' Snowdon, its closest runner-up in the alpine stakes. The climb is long and arduous—up a flinty path, up through layers of freezing cloud, past a precipice 1,500ft. deep, plummeting out of sight, to the summit. And there, when the sun breaks out again, the climber has his reward in the sight of perhaps a hundred miles of Highland peaks, rank upon serried rank, shining blue against the sky, the dark depths of Loch Ness, the silver flash of the Atlantic and a first distant glimpse of Skye. Like all Scottish mountains, Ben Nevis is for tough walkers and experienced climbers only; the earthbound must content themselves with contemplating the mountain's vast flank, for its head is generally hidden in thick cloud. I, however, have been lucky—driving south into Fort William, on a day of grey mist and thin rain, the weather suddenly lifted: a perfect rainbow arched over Loch Linnhe and to the east, the massive crest of Ben Nevis emerged from its collar of broken cloud. On this occasion, I was on my way back to London. As I sat in the station at Fort William waiting for the overnight express, I watched, not without regret, passengers in the adjacent bus depot getting aboard for what is perhaps the best of all runs to Skye. A coach leaves daily (in both directions) for Broadford and Portree, via the Kyle of Lochalsh and Kyleakin. An occasional steamer along the loch and through the Sound of Sleat makes much the same journey.

Another alternative is to travel by road or train to the little port of Mallaig. Although half a day will do to go there and back, it is well worth spending another night in Fort William to explore this reach of the coast. Mallaig is at the end of the line — the 'West Highland Railway' runs no further — and from then on, you are on your own in the northern Highlands, where narrow roads are often snowbound and the solitary traveller has to rely for shelter on the bed and breakfast accommodation provided by hospitable farmsteads.

Describing Mallaig, the well-known Scottish writer, Eric Linklater, catches its flavour perfectly: 'Mallaig, a few miles north of Morar, on the southern horn of Loch Nevis, is a fishing port whose houses, from the sea, appear to be haphazardly and a little precariously attached to a steep and sombre background; but its harbour is a robust and lively marine market, crowded with great, brown-varnished boats — broad in the beam, with a proudly rising sheer — that transfer their gleaming cargoes, among flocks of screaming sea-gulls, to lorries that nonchalantly manoeuvre on a slippery wooden pier'. Some have recorded Mallaig's variegated smells — soup and mutton, oil and sea-spray; others have detailed the scenery, the hills and rocky headlands that surround it. It has a steep main street which runs downhill to the jetty, some pubs filled to overflowing once the catch is in and safely on its way to the city, a post-office, a sea-front hotel.

Nearby Morar and its 'white sands' play their part in the historic flight of Bonnie Prince Charlie, on the run since his defeat at Culloden. From the station (the last before Mallaig on the slow train from Fort William) a short walk takes one down to the bay and its bleached sands. It is one of the loveliest spots on the coast. A stream from Loch Morar ends in a waterfall that splashes down to the beach and out to sea, and another, slightly longer walk leads upstream to the lake with its wooded islands.

The Morar river is only a mile long; the loch, at one hundred and eighty fathoms (or 1,080 feet), is the deepest freshwater loch in Scotland. It has its monster, the Beast, A' Mhorag. And it has the further distinction of having sheltered that controversial figure of the '45, Simon Lord Lovat, who hid on one of its islands after the Battle of Culloden, till he was captured and taken to London where he was eventually beheaded at the Tower. So Morar has its marvels and its memories, but it is the scenery, the rare beauty of its sands and its silver beeches that attracts its visitors. In a region of many lakes, it is one of the most enticing.

To the east of Morar, Loch Arkaig runs quietly into Loch Lochy to join the Caledonian Canal, surrounded by Scotch Pine on its west banks, with forests of oak to the east. Once, not so long ago, it was a favourite haunt of the osprey. For tourists bound for Skye, it is well worth a detour. But it is South Morar, the district of Arisaig and the Moidart peninsula which will give these travellers a foretaste of the Hebrides. Here, on this deeply indented coast, are the long stretches of white sand that run along the Atlantic shores of Lewis and Harris; here, the green machair that sweeps down to the hillside to join them. Looking

11

seawards from the small bays and the points that guard them, there are fine views of the islands of Eigg, Rum and tiny Muck, and, to the north, the distant mountain ranges of Skye itself. Here, at Arisaig, evening turns the Sound into an alchemist's crucible, sea and sky become a vast boiling cauldron where copper turns to gold in the flaming sunset.

From Mallaig itself, Armadale Castle stands across the Sound, sheltering among the stately trees planted by generations of its ancestral owners, the MacDonalds of Sleat. The castle is re-built, but its ancient timber is as fine as any in England. A twisting road and country lanes, villages and neat villas, woodland and lusher pastures give the southern coast between Armadale and Isle Ornsay a gentle character of its own, a temperate beauty far removed from the rugged splendours found further north.

It is about forty miles from Fort William to Mallaig and double that to the Kyle of Lochalsh. The road takes one — whether by car or by train — through heath and moorland under the shadow of mountain ranges. There are sudden glimpses of the lakes, Linnhe and Lochy, Morar and dark Loch Hourn, and at Glen-finnan, the moving sight of the Monument — a slender pillar on which the Prince stands tall against the sky.

At the Kyle, the ferry chugs in and out continuously across the narrow waters of the strait, and Kyleakin is clearly visible in all its detail. A double row of fishermen's cottages leads to the pier, where the locals gather to gossip as they watch the ferry make her moorings. The jetty is full, as always, with small boys, assorted dogs, bewildered sheep, with parcels to be collected and bollards and oil and rope. Across the little bay, on a grassy headland, stands a ruined castle — Castle Moil. This ancient castle served as a look-out from where watch was kept for raiding Norsemen as well as pirate bands from nearer at hand. Another tradition says it was built by the daughter of a Norse king. This princess, nicknamed 'Saucy Mary', is said to have slung a great chain across the narrows and forced all foreign ships to pay her a toll-fee before she let them sail through. The castle is now known as

12

Castle Moil, which the official guide-book translates as meaning in Gaelic the 'roofless castle'. But it was called Dunalkin, when it was the ancient stronghold of the MacKinnons — with the MacLeods and the MacDonalds, one of the island's leading families. As to Kyleakin itself, the name is said to mean 'the kyle (or strait) of Haakon'. It is derived from a tradition that in the 13th century King Haakon of Norway weighed anchor there on his way to battle — and defeat — at Largs.

With a choice of hotels and restaurants and pleasant streets to shop in, Kyleakin is as good a place as any to take a break from travelling. It is, besides, a convenient centre for visiting the south of Skye. For those wishing to continue their journey, a regular bus service runs the eight miles to Broadford, and on to the capital, Portree, 34 miles away. The road follows the island's west coast — by common consent, its most beautiful — till it opens out into Broadford Bay. The Bay, with its surrounding scenery of hill and water, is the best thing about Broadford — a largeish village straggling untidily along the road. But it has a choice of hotels and guest houses, garages and the ever-useful Tourist Office and is, besides, a good place from which to explore the east coast. An excursion of about 30 miles takes one across the island, through the crofting-township of Torrin, then round Loch Slapin, to Elgol — there to watch the waves dancing and look out to sea for another sight of the smaller islands, Rum, Eigg and Canna and off-shore Soay. A little further north, dark Loch Coruisk lies in its bed of glacial rock. Walter Scott visited 'that dread lake, with its dark ledge of barren stone' when he was staying at Dunvegan in 1814, and thought it the grandest of all Scottish lochs. As he wrote:

> 'But, be the minstrel judge, they yield the prize
> Of desert dignity to that dread shore,
> That sees grim Coolin rise, and hears Coriskin roar'.

On a fine day it may be possible to explore Coruisk by boat from Elgol, across Loch Scavaig—a double bonus as the road along the west shore of Scavaig is definitely bumpy—before turning back to Broadford and the Red Hills. These outliers of the Cuillins get their name from the reddish glow of their granite

13

rockface. They, and indeed the whole area, are dominated by Ben Na Caillich, at well over 2,000 ft. one of the island's highest peaks. On its summit stands what is said to be Scotland's tallest cairn. Under this huge pile of stones, legend has it that a Norwegian princess is buried in fulfilment of her dying wish that the winds of her native land should blow over her grave. These curious burial mounds which are a feature of Celtic countries had already been noted by that indefatigable recorder, Boswell. Crossing the wild moorland of Strath on the way to what he erratically calls 'Broadfoot' (Broadford), he writes: 'We also saw three cairns of considerable size'.

On this leg of their journey, Dr. Johnson and Boswell were entertained, 'very merrily' we are told, by one of the MacKinnons at his home in Coire Chatachan (the 18th century Corrichatachain), whose ruins can still be inspected.

This whole district of the Strath has as many beauty spots as places of historic interest. There are, for instance, the church and ancient cemetery of Kilchrist, where the 7th century Saint Maolrubha built his cell. From the nearby 'Hill of the Masses', so-called, the saint is said to have administered to the spiritual needs of his people before he built his church.

Apart from Loch Coruisk, beauty spots — as in Skye, these are unnecessarily called — here include Loch Eishort and Loch Slapin with its fine view of the hills, and down on the coast, north of Elgol and again on the way to Coruisk, the lovely beach and machair of Camasunary.

Back in Broadford — and the next stopping place on the way north is Sligachan, with the old-established Sligachan Hotel, much favoured by climbers and fly-fishers.

Now the road runs due north, through magnificent views of the Black Cuillins to the capital, Portree. Over the top of a steep hill, past the old gaol, Meall House, the town's most ancient building which now accommodates the tourist office — and there is the first sight of Portree harbour, as pretty as the many pictures which have been taken of it. Stone steps lead down from the upper town to the quayside with its neat row of cottages and little shops; a fishing smack lies alongside, a smart yacht may be in, small craft lie at anchor, and out in the roads, there are tugs and colliers. The harbour is tucked in snugly between the hills that shelter Portree on three sides and the highlands of the Isle of Raasay opposite. At night, its lights gleam through the trees on the hillside, like so many candles competing with the stars.

With something over 1500 inhabitants, Portree has all the usual amenities: hotels to rest the weary, restaurants to feed the hungry, churches of various denominations for Sabbath observers, shops for trippers in search of souvenirs. It has, too, a main square with a police-station and a sweet-smelling bakery where relays of fresh bread and baps and scones and griddle-cakes, are baked on the premises throughout the day. As you wait for the local bus, you will hear mainly Gaelic spoken and you will feel you are truly in Skye.

As the whole world knows, it was in Portree that Bonnie Prince Charlie parted from Flora MacDonald. But its name has been taken to mean 'Port Royal' and to commemorate a much older event — the visit paid there in 1540 by King James V of Scotland. The authorities now tell us, however, that its Gaelic form of Port Righ means no more than 'the harbour on the hill slope'. Its inner loch, whose sandy shore is screened by thick sedge, is called after St. Columba who is believed to have built a chapel on an island in the lake.

From Portree onwards, the traveller has a final journey to make, diagonally across the northern peninsula, to Uig and further adventure on Harris and in the Outer Hebrides.

To end this short introduction to Skye, here is a short summary of **the best ways of getting there:**

From London (King's Cross Station) to Glasgow, then (a) by the coast road through Oban to Fort William, Mallaig or Kyle of Lochalsh. This is the route followed by the West Highlands Scenic Railway which runs as far as Mallaig. Or (b) along the banks of Loch Lomond and over Glencoe. This is the most attractive route from Edinburgh and the south-east coast of Scotland. For travellers from further north (Perth, Aberdeen and Inverness), through the Great Glen by Loch Ness to Kyle of Lochalsh, or by train from Inverness to the Kyle. A slightly shorter route leads through Invermoriston, Clunnie and Glen Shiel to Glenelg for the crossing to Kylerhea. Before the railway ran up the coast, this was the only crossing available, but it has now lost some of its popularity.

Crossings: Mallaig to Armadale
Kyle of Lochalsh to Kyleakin
Glenelg to Kylerhea
Fort William to Portree by boat: occasionally, weekday service only

The ferry at Kyle of Lochalsh operates every day, with a modified service on Sunday, when other services are closed. For up-to-date itineraries, including mini-cruises, consult the local offices of Caledonian-MacBrayne, who operate practically all the services to the islands. British Rail also supply information about crossings.

A few **suggested excursions** from the landing stages:

1)   At **Armadale** the main road (851) ends, but there is a good secondary road running south some five miles to the Aird of Sleat, through Ardvasar, Caligarry and Tormore. From there a footpath leads on to the Point of Sleat, the southern tip of Skye. Turning north along the 851 the road runs up to Broadford, through the pretty villages of Camuscross and Isle Ornsay to Kinloch. On a fine day the first part of the journey affords fine views of the Scottish coast across the Sound of Sleat. From Isle Ornsay, the road skirts Loch na Dalash and runs through the woods of Duisdale. A distance of approximately 15 miles.

2)   From **Kyleakin** it is eight miles to Broadford. Take the coast road (850) which runs west through moorland overshadowed

by hills and flanked seawards by the Inner Sound of Minch. At Lusa, the mountain road from **Kylerhea** comes in. It is a steep narrow road which climbs through Glen Arroch. A safe road, well maintained, but diagreeable driving in wet weather. From Lusa, the 850 runs on through the old crofting villages of Breakish, Scullamus and Harrapool, now growing sadly derelict since fishing left the coast.

3)   From **Broadford** west to Elgol. At the Broadford Hotel, the 881 meets the 850. It runs due west along Loch Kilchrist to Kilbride and Torrin, then round Loch Slapin and south across Strathaird to the upland village of Elgol on Loch Scavaig. Tracks not suitable for cars lead down to the beaches from Elgol and further up the shore of Loch Scavaig, from Camasunary.

On the way back to Broadford, it is wise to take the same road: the narrow roads which cross Strathaird and further east, run along the Red Hills, are hardly more than tracks best left to walkers. The round tour from Broadford to Elgol and back: about 30 miles but allow time to walk down to the beaches and, in good weather, visit Loch Coruisk by motor boat.

DUNTULM CASTLE

A Chapter on Castles

High up in the north-west corner of Skye stands Dunvegan Castle, where it has stood for 700 years and more. This ancestral seat of Clan MacLeod is undoubtedly the island's main tourist attraction: of the 600,000 visitors who take the ferry to Kyleakin every year — with a quarter of a million cars between them — most take the road to Dunvegan.

Once it was not possible to do so — until late in the 17th century, when the MacLeod of the day built a flight of steps for the convenience of his guests, the castle could be approached only by boat across the waters of the bay. During the reign, if such it can be called, of Rorie More, who earned his nickname of Great Roderick for his spirit rather than his stature, the castle was still surrounded on three sides by water and on the fourth by wild moorland, making it a well-nigh impregnable fortress. Entrance to the castle was by a sea-gate which is said to have been built by the founder of the family in 1270. This was Leod, son of the King of Man, who came across the waters to marry the heiress of the MacRails who then held Dunvegan. From Leod, are descended the MacLeods of Skye, as well as the junior branch, the MacLeods of Lewis. The chiefly title of the MacLeod of MacLeod is held by the senior branch, of the House of Harris and Dunvegan.

Through the ages, Dunvegan Castle has stood safe from attack by pirates as well as from frequent raids and depredations by

18

rival clans. Today it is completely renovated without and modernised within, and to get an idea of what it was like, we must turn once more to the 'Journey to the Western Islands of Scotland'. There, at the end of the 18th century, Dr. Johnson was writing: 'Dunvegan is a rocky prominence, that juts out into a bay, on the west side of Sky. The House, which is the principal seat of MacLeod, is partly old and partly modern; it is built upon the rock, and looks upon the water. It forms two sides of a small square: on the third side is the skeleton of a castle of unknown antiquity, supposed to have been a Norwegian fortress, when the Danes were master of the Islands . . . This house was accessible only from the water, until the last possessor opened an entrance by stairs upon the land'. Boswell follows this description closely: 'The great size of the castle, which is partly old, partly new, and is built upon a rock close to the sea, while the land around it presents nothing but wild, moorish, hilly and craggy appearances, gave a rude magnificence to the scene. Having dismounted, we ascended a flight of steps, which was made by the late MacLeod, for the accommodation of persons coming to him by land, there formerly being, for security, no other access to the castle but from the sea; so that visitors who came by the land were under the necessity of getting a boat, and sailed round to the only place where it could be approached'.

A curious legend concerns the rebuilding of the Castle: it was said that whoever started it would not live to see the work finished. Of one laird who undertook some renovation, we are told: 'he desisted in a little time, and put his money to worse use', presumably on the green baize of London's fashionable gaming tables. However, modern Dunvegan as it now stands is very much in business as one of the oldest inhabited castles in Scotland, and its long-lived owners are thriving. Dame Flora MacLeod died in 1976 at the age of 98. She was buried to the lament of the pipers in Dunvegan cemetery, where many of her famous forbears lie at rest. The previous chief of the clan — the 23rd MacLeod of MacLeod — lived well past his 80th year. But legends are stubborn in the Highlands. Hard facts dissolve in the mist over the hills, and the Fairy Flag flies on.

The Flag is now a fragile fold of embroidered silk, which may have been a Saracen banner brought home from the Crusades. But others say it comes from fairyland, where its pattern was worked by the elves. One legend has it that it was handed over to the MacLeods to save the day during a clash of the clans at Fairy Bridge nearby. Another story goes that while an infant MacLeod was left unattended, the fairies stole his swaddling clothes and returned him to his cradle wrapped in the Fairy Flag. As in all the best fairy tales, the flag has magic powers: when it is waved, it will grant the MacLeods three wishes, or save them from three dangers. Twice already it has been put to the test — during a raid, it brought defeat to a far superior force of MacDonalds and it put an end to a cattle plague. The next, and last, time it is waved, it will crumble away and vanish. A curse attends it: if it is waved frivolously, the heir to the MacLeods will die.

The stories that surround the MacLeod's Fairy Flag illustrate the nature of the Scottish fairyland. Here are no merry sprites dancing in the sunny glades of the Forest of Arden. Celtic fairies are cruel, treacherous and rather frightening, far nearer to the terrible trolls of Scandinavian mythology than to Merrie England's Puck and Ariel and Mustardseed. Some can be seduced into co-operating — both Browny and the Old Man with the Long Beard, Greogach in Gaelic, respond to a regular diet of milk and in return help with the chores. But on the whole, it is wiser not to meddle, or like the two musicians who played to the fairies as they danced in the Tomnahurich cemetery, you may be carried away for 100 years. In this Inverness version of Rip van Winkle, when the ball was over, the two men made their way back to town where people pointed at them and jeered at the strange fashion of their clothes, which were, indeed, a century out of date. In the Hebrides, a spirit lurks under the waves to overturn the fishing boats in high seas, while in calm weather the seal woman sings siren songs to lure the sailors into her power. The 'muckle back devil' with his handmaidens, the witches, is everywhere. And when the mists envelop Skye, you don't need the Celtic 'second sight' to hear the Taischs speaking,

or to see their disembodied spirits wander round Dunvegan cemetery. Boswell gives an instance of these curious manifestations.
It was told him while he was staying at Kingsburgh House as
it befell Old Kingsburgh himself one day when he was riding
in Skye. 'Some women, who were at work in a field on the side
of the road said to him they had heard two taischs (that is, the
voices of two people about to die) and what was remarkable,
one of them was an *English* taisch, which they had never heard
before. When he returned, he at that very place met two funerals,
and one of them was that of a woman who had come from the
mainland, and could speak only English'. Coincidence to the
pragmatist, but when darkness falls on the moor, such ghostly
tales seem less fanciful and it is comforting to seek refuge in
the Castle where the red mahogany gleams in the firelight and
rows of MacLeods look down from the oak-panelled walls.

Painted by the Scottish artists, Allan Ramsay (1713-1794) and
Sir Henry Raeburn\ (1756-1823), in their finery of flowing lace
and tartan waistcoat, with gold buttons and button-holes, with
plaid and kilt and tartan hose, some in powdered wigs and some
in their hair, wearing the cockaded bonnet, with their wives
elegant in white satin, several generations of MacLeods in their
gilded frames portray that unique social phenomenon — the
Scottish laird.

The laird, who owned the castles and the land, as well as the
people who lived on it, administered the clan system which
was tribal as much as feudal and which lived on in the Highlands for several hundred years after it had vanished from the
rest of the British Isles. Within the 'hereditary jurisdictions'
(which were not abolished until 1748) he had the right of life
and death over his tenants, and there was in practice no appeal
from his private court. His clansmen served him as a standing
private army — he could call them out to fight for whatever
cause he happened to favour. As Dr. Johnson put it: 'He told
them to whom they should be friends or enemies, what King
they should obey, and what religion they should profess.' Any
attempt to resist was swiftly punished: the refractory clansman's

21

home and his crops were burned and his animals turned loose. In exchange for his total submission, the laird protected him and leased him the land from which he scratched a living. How the bargain worked out in practice varied from laird to laird — one could be as a well loved father to the clansmen who bore his surname; another would exploit his tenantry ruthlessly to his own advantage and that of his close kinsmen and most favoured retainers who formed a small court, surrounded him and accompanied him everywhere. But whatever the nature of their rule, tyrannical or paternalistic, all the Highland lairds were forced in some measure to share their tenants' poverty in a country where the soil was naturally poor and methods of culture, primitive. The produce of the kail-yard, where cabbages grew with perhaps a few rows of peas and beans, was shared by castle and croft alike. It has been estimated that the Highland lairds lived on one-tenth of the income enjoyed by similar ranks of the English squirearchy, while the so-called 'bonnet lairds' of the 18th century supported themselves and their families on a rent-roll of £20 a year and the meagre harvest of the 'home field' (that is, the bit of land immediately adjoining the homestead). But whatever their income, the lairds had in common with the tenantry a pride of clan which sprung from the long memory of old feuds and battles fought in common. They were treated by their peasants with a lack of subservience, a proud familiarity which astonished English travellers, especially as it was seen in contrast to the rigid and complicated etiquette which ruled elsewhere within the social system.

Taking, for instance, the question of the commonly-held surname, strict rules governed the correct form of address: the chief of the clan was called by the surname only, The MacLeod. Though he had no title, to call him plain Mister would have been to degrade him from his acknowledged rank of tribal chief. His principal tenants, the tacksmen, were named after their lands, such as Kingsburgh, and their wives, addressed as Mistress, were accepted as being 'ladies'. Other gentlemen of landed property were called after their estates, Raasay, for instance. This custom led to a comic quandary for the unfortunate owner of the Isle of Muck, which lies off Eigg beyond the Cuillin Sound. This gentleman is reported to have tried again and again to get the name of his tiny dominion changed to the more euphonious Monk. All his efforts having failed, he insisted thereafter on being addressed by the full appellation of Isle of Muck — an understandable if clumsy compromise.

That the social system of the Highlands should have survived pretty well intact until the Industrial Revolution can be explained only by their isolation. Towards the end of the reign of George the First, an early English traveller, Edward Burt, wrote: 'The Highlands are little known even to the inhabitants of the low country of Scotland, for they have ever dreaded the difficulties and dangers of travelling among the mountains; and when some extraordinary occasion has obliged any of them to make such a progress he has generally speaking made his testament before he set out, as though he were entering on a long and dreaded sea voyage, wherein it was very doubtful if he should ever return. But to the people of England, except some few and those chiefly the soldiers, the Highlands are hardly known at all; for there has been less written on the subject than of the Indies.' Even James the First, the first King to reign over both England and Scotland, went no further north than Dundee when he revisited his native land towards the end of his life. In 1707, more than a hundred years after the accession to the joint throne of the Stuart King, the Treaty of Union gave Queen Anne rather more purchase over her northern subjects. Under its provisions, the two nations, now united under the name of Great Britain, were represented by a single Parliament. Both its Houses were enlarged, with another 45 Scottish members sitting in the Commons and 16 Scottish peers in the House of Lords. Trade rights were thrown open and a common coinage adopted. Queen Anne sent out a proclamation: 'I desire and expect from my subjects of both nations that from henceforth they act with all possible respect and kindness to one another, that so it may appear to all the world they have their hearts disposed to become one people.'

The Lowlands and the Border country, which profited most

from the new preferential trade terms, responded eagerly. But the Highlands kept their distance. The first rapprochement came a generation later when General Wade bridged the river Spean near Fort William and cut a road towards Inverness. This bridge is described by the Welsh naturalist, Thomas Pennant, whose book 'Tour in Scotland' came out in 1771, two years before Dr. Johnson and Boswell set off for the Highlands and the Hebrides. 'High-Bridge, a fine bridge of three arches flung over the torrent Spean, founded on rocks; two of the arches are 95 feet high. This bridge was built by General Wade, in order to form a communication with the country'. His purpose was, in fact, to facilitate the movement of troops in pursuit of rebellious Highlanders, but in effect the new bridge and the first roads that were built opened up the territory to travellers from the south. It was to be another 20 years or so, however, before the Highlands started to conform with the rest of Scotland and to adopt something of the English way of life. That was after the hopes of the Stuarts had been finally crushed in the rebellion of 1745 and repressive laws had deprived the Highlands of many of their ancient customs. 'The rebellion was a disorder violent in its operation, but salutary in its effects', says Thomas Pennant. The Industrial Revolution eventually brought new wealth and finished what Culloden had begun.

It was poverty as much as isolation, which kept the Highlands and Western Islands in their old ways. And this poverty is bleakly illustrated by the ruined castles of Skye.

Dunvegan has survived and opens its panelled warmth to the tourist. Elsewhere, the wind blows free through the empty shells of ancient fortresses. One such, Castle Camus, in the south of the island, has earned itself the name of Caisteal Uaine, which means the Green Castle in Gaelic, for there is nothing there now but a grassy mound and crumbling walls covered with ivy. In its time, it has borne several names: Knock Castle, Castle of the Bay, and an old chronicler records it as one of 'Twa strenthie castells in Slait, ye ane callit Castell Chammes'. Not much is known of its long history: it was once a stronghold of the power-

24

ful Clan Ranald and there is some documentary evidence that
it was occupied in the 17th century by Sir Donald MacDonald
of Sleat. The castle was frequently under attack by the MacLeods
and here legend makes up for what history omits. During one
attack, the besiegers were driven back and the castle was saved
by Mary MacDonald, whose heroic feats survive in Gaelic song.
Another legendary story tells how John Ban MacPherson defended
it single-handed against a raid from Dunvegan. Whether or not
he really did carry out these military exploits, John Ban Mac-
Pherson will achieve a small measure of fame as the progenitor
of a distinguished clerical dynasty, which included the 18th
century minister of Sleat, Dr. Martin MacPherson, who entertained Johnson and Boswell at Ostaig, nearby. Boswell had a
good opinion of Dr. Martin — 'his manners and address pleased
us much'. But he thought less of another member of the family,
one Dr. MacPherson whose 'Dissertations on the Ancient Cale-
donians' he perused one rainy day at Corrichatachain. He thought
them fanciful, 'unsatisfactory conjectures as to antiquity, before
the days of records'.

But when we cross Sleat to Tokavaig to visit the second of Clan
Ranald's 'strenthie castells', Dunscaith, it is largely to fancy
that we must turn again. Here, at Dunscaith, the mythologies
of Ireland and Scotland combine to tell us that it was the warrior
Queen of Skye, Sgatach, who gave her name to the castle (dun =
stronghold). There she was visited by Cuchullin himself who came
from Ireland to learn the arts of war from her. She taught him
all she knew, as well as how to play the harp, and the legendary
tribal king of Ulster fell in love with the Queen of the Isles. The
few ruins that are left standing on the rocky promontory do no
more than hint at Castle Dunscaith's ancient power and compass.
Forty feet above Loch Eishort, it is isolated from the mainland
by a wide chasm which was once spanned by a drawbridge. There
are vestiges of its barbican and of the flight of stone steps which
led up to the castle's main gate. Recent archaeological exploration
in the vicinity also suggests that the shore — with its lovely stretch
of sands at Tarskavaig — as well as the moorland have been inhabited from the earliest recorded times. Two cairns stand nearby at

Inver Aulavaig, south of the small town of Ord. The largest measures 18ft in diameter and when it was opened up, was found to contain a stone cist. These coffins called cists, made of hollowed stone or a tree-trunk dug out, are associated in the Hebrides with the Vikings.

Spare historical records put MacDonald chieftains in Dunscaith in the Middle Ages — when they built the great baronial hall whose foundations are still visible on the far point of the promontory and, presumably, the prison in the corner of the courtyard. There they stayed until early in the 17th century. Then, in 1616, or thereabouts, they removed to the north, to their stronghold of Duntulm. There is no given explanation for their removing in this way, but it seems likely that they wanted to strengthen their hold over the Trotternish peninsula, whose ownership was contended by the MacLeods. The dispute was eventually resolved in favour of the MacDonalds, provided they settled in the territory. A directive of the Privy Council, in the reign of James I, orders MacDonald of Sleat to 'Mak his duelling and residence at Duntullm' and with 'all convenient diligence prepair materialls and cause build ane civile and comelie hous, and if his hous be decayit that he sall repair and mend the same'. After the first Jacobite rebellion in 1715, however, the Mac-Donalds were no longer able to carry out this last clause. Their chief had taken up the cause of the Stuart Pretender, severely reduced his income in the process and eventually forfeited the Clan Ranald estates. A hundred years before, when the Mac-Donalds had moved into Duntulm, their wealth had been ample to transform what was probably no more than a small fort, one of those ancient and primitive structures known as 'duns' which still remain scattered over Skye. The old watchtower was built on, enlarged and made more inhabitable, until, by the 1650s, it may well have rivalled the comforts of Dunvegan. Its short period of pride came to an end with the Rebellion. In its aftermath, the servants were dismissed and eventually Sir Alexander MacDonald took his household back south to Monkstadt (or Mugshot), leaving Duntulm to the erosion of the wind and the waves.

But tradition supplies its own explanation for Duntulm's fate: legend says that before Duntulm was abandoned, an infant Mac-Donald, some say the heir, fell from a window to his death on the rocks below. His father took a horrible revenge by seizing the child's nursemaid and setting her adrift in a small, oarless boat. There are many reports of ghostly hauntings at Duntulm, but perhaps it was conscience which in the end drove the Mac-Donalds away from this scene of their tragedy and crime.

There is another of their castles in this part of the island — very much MacDonald territory — and the groves the keels of their galleys wore into the rocky foreshore are still clearly marked. It was built in 1580 by Hugh MacDonald, a nephew of the then MacDonald of Sleat, by the banks of Loch Snizort and is known as Caisteal Uisdean, or Hugh's Castle. But it probably pre-dated him and, like Duntulm, may once have been a simple keep which grew with its owner's prosperity. This Hugh MacDonald, who was known as 'the son of Archibald the Cleric', came to a dread-ful end, and provided Duntulm with another of its ghosts. Hugh's uncle and chief took exception to his setting up in his own castle and imprisoned him in the dungeon of Duntulm, leaving him to perish insane on a diet of saltbeef and sea-water. Round all the castles in Skye, there is woven a tale of heroic deeds and dreadful revenge. But ruins are now the only record left of their ancient and blood-thirsty history.

On his first visit to the Highlands, the traveller from the south may be surprised, and disappointed, to find none of the stately homes and fine mansions that abound in the English countryside. There, the 18th century was a period of peace and attendant plenty — at any rate, for the upper classes — and a sound economy resulted in what we now would call a building boom. Architecture flourished: great noblemen, gentlemen of landed property, merchants en-riched by their trade with the Indies vied with each other in building, rebuilding, improving, restoring fine homes of which elegance was the keynote. They preserved their woods, land-scaped their gardens, contrived ornamental lakes and waterfalls, planted orchards and bosquets and noble avenues of beech and

27

elm and oak for their sons and grandsons to enjoy. There was time enough and to spare when it seemed in England that peace would last forever.

In Scotland, 400 years of intermittent warfare with the English had not only left the country impoverished and isolated; it had instilled in the Scots a deep aversion to the English way of life. They had no wish to emulate the graceful achievements of their southern neighbours, whom they regarded as purse-proud and overbearing. Besides, the native rugged pride of the Highlander, and to some extent the rigidity of Calvinistic doctrine, combined to create a climate averse to such refinements. As long as the 'fiery cross' rallied the clans across the moors, to spend time on embellishing the manse would have been regarded as effeminate. Above all, there was no money to waste.

The last years of the reign of William III, saw a natural calamity which devastated the countryside and was not to be repeated in severity until the potato famine of 1846. During these 'dear years' as they came to be known, there were six consecutive seasons of disastrous weather when no harvest ripened, the crofters died of hunger and their landlords' rent-rolls suffered in proportion. In the reign of Queen Anne, the harvest failed again — villages and hamlets were deserted and beggars filled the roads. Then came the two risings of 1715 and 1745 when the Jacobites in Scotland paid dear for their allegiance to the Stuart cause. Some were executed, many more went into exile and forfeited their estates. These were already depleted by the cost of raising and maintaining troops to fight the Hanoverian forces. In battle, many of the clansmen fell and this loss of manpower further impoverished land which had been left to the care of the womenfolk ever since the call had gone out to rally to the Pretenders.

Yet, with their French connection and often Catholic background, which made them immune from the rigidities of John Knox's social discipline, the Highland Jacobites would have responded more readily to the refinements which England was introducing. Accustomed as many of them were to the magnificence of life in the French chateaux, they would have been very much at home amid the splendours of Blenheim or Houghton. As it was, there was more pleasure and freedom than elsewhere in Scotland in a Jacobite household, but the house itself, for lack of money, appeared as grim as any other. 'Tall, stone mansions, each with its corbel-stepped gable roof, stood up gaunt and fortress-like in the treeless and peopleless landscape', writes the historian, G.M. Trevelyan. 'Many of these country houses had grown up by the clumsy additions to the war-towers of former days. There was seldom any window on the exposed north side, even when it commanded the best and only view of the landscape. The days of lawns, avenues and walled gardens was yet to come. The farm buildings, with their heady smells and litter, abutted on the mansion; the cornfields came up to the walls on one side, and on another was an ill-kept garden of kale, physic-herbs and native flowers.' It is only in the Scottish Lowlands that classical mansions attempt to rival the stately homes south of the border, and the amateur of 18th century architecture should travel no further north.

But if the ages of Queen Anne and the Georges passed over the Highlands and Islands without leaving their mark, the buildings of older times are amply represented. Some of the medieval watch-towers, as we have seen, became fortified castles; others still stand solitary along the coast and on the moorland, and apart from the ancient duns, there are fine examples of the more elaborate brochs. In place-names in particular, the two are often confused, but the distinction between them is clearly made by the late historian and archaeologist, W. Douglas Simpson.

'By *duns,* we mean primitive fortifications consisting of one or more ramparts of loose stone, following the contours of the site, and usually enclosing hut circles. A *broch* is just a highly specialised form of dun. It is a circular tower of dry-built masonry, enclosing an open court. The thick wall is hollowed out with galleries, and a circular stair winds round the tower to the parapet. Round the inside there was, in some cases, a kind of penthouse, supported on posts. Many brochs have outbuildings clustered round them, usually within a defensive rampart.' One of the oldest brochs, Dun-an-Iarhard, stands on the shore of Loch Dunvegan, about a mile north of the Castle. How old it is we cannot tell, but in it was found a votive offering — a baked clay model of a bale of goods designed to propitiate the gods by some Roman merchant on the dangerous voyage to the Hebrides. Though the Romans never occupied Scotland, here is extra proof that their mariners sought trade even as far as the Western Isles. And it is well worth crossing back to the mainland to visit the notable brochs near Glenelg. It is a lovely walk up to Dun Telve and Dun Trodan, through fine wooded scenery, along a rocky ravine where in season rhododendrons and wild roses clamber among the boulders. Both brochs are carefully preserved and still stand to a height of some thirty feet. Further up on the hillside, there is a neolithic chambered cairn, Balvraid, which was excavated in 1965.

Another pleasant island walk, this time from Portree, takes one to the old hill-fort of Dun Gerashader, perched on a rocky outcrop between the road and the sea. The line of its four ramparts, built of boulders set end to end, is still clearly defined; within the enclosure, there are the remains of hut circles. Once this fort protected a sizeable community; now it is inhabited by three fairy cows and their supernatural herdsman.

But the finest dun on Skye is undoubtedly Dun Beag, in the Bracadale district. Built of basalt blocks, it survives to a height of 12ft in scenery so spectacular that even Boswell, like his contemporaries no lover of nature untrammelled, was moved to describe it, as sea and land spread out before him from the top of the ruined tower: 'There is an extensive view of Loch Braccadil and, at a distance, of the isles of Barra and South Uist; and, on the landside, the Cuillin, a prodigious range of mountains, capped with rocky pinnacles in a strange variety of shapes'. The ages have passed over Dun Beag . . . excavators have turned up objects as disparate as a bronze buckle and a gold ring from the days of the Vikings as well as coins minted over 700 years ago, the earliest dating from the reign of Henry II. But the landscape has not changed and the view is as Boswell saw it on Wednesday 22nd September 1773.

Car Excursions

One can easily visit Skye's two main castles — Dunvegan and Duntulm — in the course of half a day's driving, but it is probably more rewarding to make a separate excursion to each, spending time exploring the shores of Loch Dunvegan and the Bracadale district, and from Duntulm, seeing the Flora MacDonald sites — Monkstadt, Kingsburgh, Kilmuir and, perhaps, Flodigarry.

Dunvegan: From Portree, the A850 leads through Skeabost across the narrow neck of Trotternish, then along Snizort Beag and over to the shores of Loch Greshornish, through Edinbain to the Fairy Bridge, then due south, with a sharp turn east to Dunvegan village, past the cemetery, itself well worth a stop. An alternative road, the 863, for the return trip leads south-east to Bracadale, then turning due east runs along Glen Drynoch to Sligachan, where it rejoins the 850. Turn north to the left for Portree, and continue due east for Sconser and Broadford.

Duntulm: Uig, where the 856 ends, is the nearest township for Duntulm. From there the 855 runs due north up to Kilmuir, then along Score Bay. Some of the most beautiful scenery is on the road home, where the 855 crosses the point of Trotternish to Flodigarry, then runs south through Staffin along the coast, past the Kilt rocks and the Storr down to Portree. For a short cut from Uig take the road to Staffin which climbs past waterfalls to cross the ridge of the Quiraing and comes out at the village of Brogaig on the west coast, south of Flodigarry. **Hugh's Castle** lies off the 856 between Uig and Borve. At Hinnisdale Bridge a rough road, best walked, leads down to the shores of Loch Snizort, a few miles north of Kingsburgh.

The dramatic ruins of **Dunscaith,** in the south of the country are best reached from Broadford, taking the 851 through Camuscross, then turning right, west, across Sleat to Ord. From here

31

a good secondary road runs the three or four miles to Tokavaig, the nearest parking point to the castle on the coast. **Dun Beag** overlooks the 863 by the village of Struan and is within a short walk from Bracadale. The town itself is at the junction of the 863 from Sligachan and a good cross country road from Portree. **Dun an Iarhard** lies by the north shore of Loch Dunvegan; Dun Gerashader is a couple of miles north of Portree off the 855.

Prince Errant

1745 — and a proclamation is given out 'at Whitehall, the first day of August'. It reads: 'We have received information that the eldest son of the Pretender did lately embark in France in order to land in some part of his Majesty's kingdoms. We, being moved with just indignation at so daring an attempt, do hereby, in his Majesty's name, command and require all his Majesty's officers, civil and military, and all other of his Majesty's loving subjects, to use their utmost endeavours to seize and secure the said son of the Pretender whenever he shall land, or attempt to land, or be found in Great Britain or Ireland . . . in order to his being brought to justice.' The hunt for Bonnie Prince Charlie was on.

The proclamation continues, for the benefit of his Hanoverian Majesty's 'loving subjects', 'to the intent that all due encouragement shall be given to so important a service, we do hereby further, in his Majesty's name, promise a reward of thirty-thousand pounds to such person or persons who shall seize and secure the said son of the said Pretender'.

The bribe offered is now worth about half-a-million pounds. In the Highlands, where the well-to-do lived on an income of a few hundred a year, while their fellow countrymen, fighting a never-ending battle against inclement weather and unresponsive soil, handled groats rather than guineas, it was worth far more than a king's ransom. Who then was this expensive fugitive?

He was: 'Charles Edward Louis Philippe Casimir Stuart, born in Rome on 20th December, 1720, the son of James Edward Stuart, and the Princess Clementina Sobieska of Poland, a granddaughter of the great John Sobieski who saved Europe from the Turks. James Edward Stuart, the Old Pretender, was the only surviving son of James II, King of England, Scotland and Ireland, who died in 1701. After his death, James Edward was acclaimed as James III by his Jacobite adherents and Louis XIV of France', writes Eric Linklater.

When the proclamation went out from Whitehall, the Young Pretender, as Hanoverians and historians called him, had already landed in Scotland. From the French brig, Du Teillay, which carried 44 guns, he disembarked at Loch Nan Uamh, near Arisaig, on 25th July 1745. On the 19th August, the royal standard was unfurled at Glenfinnan and James again proclaimed King (with Prince Charles as his Regent). The ceremony, which took place on the beach at Glenfinnan — where the Monument now stands — was followed, we are told, 'by a general Housaw, and a great deal of Allacrity', no doubt helped on by the casks of brandy which the Prince had ordered to be distributed so that his men could drink the health of their true King.

The men may have huzza-ed merrily, but their chiefs were less sanguine. Soon after landing, the Prince had sent to Skye, but the response from both Sir Alexander MacDonald of Sleat and from The MacLeod of MacLeod was disappointing, though hardly surprising.

The Stuart claim to the throne was dynastically impeccable: from James the First (the sixth of Scotland) it had come down from father to son in direct line. After the Restoration and the death of his brother, Charles the Second, James the Second was deposed and succeeded by William, Prince of Orange, who as King William, reigned jointly with his wife, Mary. She and her sister Anne, who succeeded the royal pair, were both daughters of James the Second by his first wife, Anne Hyde. As for the Hanoverian monarchs, what Stuart blood, already diluted, still ran in their veins came from the distaff side, through Charles the First's sister, Elizabeth, and her daughter, Sophia, who married the Elector Palatine and bore him George the First. The latter's arrival in England in the late summer of 1714 and his feelings as he surveyed his new kingdom are perfectly captured by the late Winston Churchill. 'Here on English soil stood an unprepossessing figure, an obstinate and humdrum German martinet with dull brains and coarse tastes. As a commander in the late wars, he had been sluggish and incompetent, and as a ruler of men, he had shown no quickening ability or generosity of spirit. Yet the rigidity of his mind was relieved by a slow shrewdness and a brooding common-sense. The British throne was no easy inheritance, especially for a foreign prince. King George took it up grudgingly, and it was ungraciously that he played his allotted part. He owed his crown to the luck of circumstance, but he never let it slip from his grasp.' The son of this unattractive foreigner was a man of the same stamp, and the Scots knew it. The Scottish poet, Allan Cunningham, was not born until 1784, but his ballad entitled 'The Wee, wee German Lairdie' no doubt reflects accurately enough what the Highlanders of the '45 felt about this king whom the poet calls the 'princeling of the cabbage patch'.

'What the de'il hae we got for a King,
But a wee, wee German lairdie!
An' whan we gaed to bring him hame,
He was delving in his kail-yardie.
An' he's clapt down in our gudeman's chair
The wee, wee German lairdie
. . . An' he's pu'd the rose of English lowns (fellows)
An' brak' the harp of Irish clowns,
But our thistle will jag his thumbs,
The wee, wee German lairdie'

George the Second is then invited to come and test the metal of the Jacobites' longswords:

'Come up among the Highland hills,
Thou wee, wee German lairdie;
. . . Our hills are steep, our glens are deep
Nae fitting for a yardie
An' we've the trenching blades of weir (war)
Wad twine ye o' yere German gear;
An' pass ye 'neath the claymore's shear
Thou feckless German lairdie.'

As we have seen, Prince Charles Edward was no Pretender, a word which, in any case, Boswell for one was to reject from his vocabulary. As he wrote: 'It may be a Parliamentary expression, but it is not a *gentlemanly* expression'. However, for the gentry of the Highlands and the Islands there were other considerations than the soundness of the blood royal, and not least among them, the urgent need as the summer advanced to get the harvest in. On it, both man and master depended for his livelihood. Besides, to the cautious at any rate, the Prince's endeavour must have seemed desperate. The King of France, Louis XIV, who was at war with England, had promised support, and indeed a French invasion fleet had been made ready. But a freak gale destroyed it off Dunkirk and it was not replaced. From then on, pleas for money, men or munitions were largely ignored.

Yet the old Jacobite cause had its appeal, especially for the Catholics who were well represented in the Highlands and in the Hebrides. Many of the Highland families had taken up the Stuart cause from the start, some had already fought in 1715 and forfeited their estates and most were too deeply compromised in Hanoverian circles to turn back. Many were better acquainted with the French court at St. Germain — the traditional refuge of Stuart exiles — than with their own moors. And there was always the temptation to have another go at such hereditary enemies as the Duke of Argyll's hated Campbells.

In the event, the Stuart forces are thought to have numbered 5000 men and 600 horse. But estimates vary, and some put the total at no more than 2500 men at the most. The clans who had rallied, as listed by the Scottish writer, Andrew Lang, included: 'MacDonalds of all septs, Camerons, Atholl men, Stewarts of Appin, MacGregors, Perth's regiment, MacLachlans, Nairn's band, and a few Lowland gentry and their servants.' In this list, Skye was, of course, represented by the MacDonalds.

The campaign started off well. There was a quick victory at Prestonpans, on the Firth of Forth, and the road to Edinburgh, not ten miles west, lay open. Edinburgh surrendered, though the Castle garrison held out. Leaving it to its own devices, the Prince and his men marched in. He spent the autumn in the Scottish capital, issued a few good-natured proclamations, made a few new recruits, raised levies and bought boots for his barefoot Highlanders. Every night he dined in public and gave balls where he was surrounded and feted by the ladies of the town, though it is said that he himself did not dance. The Young Chevalier was everyone's darling. An English spy in Edinburgh for his masters described the Prince's appearance: 'The young Chevalier is about five foot eleven inches high, very proportionably made; wears his own hair, has a full forehead, a small but lively eye, a round brown-complexioned face; nose and mouth pretty small; full under the chin; not a long neck; under his jaw a pretty many pimples. He is always in a Highland habit, as are all about him. When I saw him, he had a short Highland plaid waistcoat; breeches of the same, a blue garter on, and a St. Andrew's Cross, hanging by a green ribbon at his button-hole.' Court painters leave out pimples, but in every other respect, this description tallies with the many portraits of the Prince.

On the first of November, the small Stuart army moved off to cross the border; through Carlisle and Manchester, they got as far south as Swarkstone Bridge, six miles beyond Derby. There, on the 4th of December, they were defeated by a force double their number under the command of the King's son, the young Duke of Cumberland, and London heaved a sigh of relief. From then on, their road led back due north to Inverness and Drumossie Moor where, in the grim battle of Culloden, the Stuart forces were routed and the Stuart cause lost for good.

Much is still being written about the severity or otherwise of English reprisals, but there is no doubt that at Culloden, Cumberland earned his nickname of 'The Butcher'. Prisoners were shot out of hand, the wounded killed off — clubbed or bayonetted where they lay — the fugitives pursued relentlessly and their families harrassed. A stone on the desolate moor marks 'the graves of the gallant Highlanders who fought for Scotland and Prince Charlie' on 16th April 1746. Among them were the 120 men brought over from Skye by The MacKinnon of MacKinnon.

The Prince now took the 'road to the isles' in the greatest man-hunt ever recorded, and it was left to the poets to suggest the damage he had done. One old folk-ballad Robert Burns made his own:

> 'The lovely lass o' Inverness
> Nae joy nor pleasure can she see;
> For e'en and morn she cries, Alas!
> And ay the saut (salt) tear blin's her e'e:
> Drumossie moor, Drumossie day,
> A woeful day it was to me;
> For there I lost a father dear,
> My father dear and brethren three!
> Their winding-sheet the bluddy clay
> Their graves are growing green to see;
> And by them lies the dearest lad
> That ever blessed a woman's e'e!'

After many adventures and vicissitudes all borne cheerfully, the royal fugitive reached Skye, where he landed on June 29th under the guidance of the island's heroine, Flora MacDonald. The little party, which included Flora's manservant, Neil MacKinnon, and six rowers, had set out the previous night from Rossinish on Benbecula, where the Prince, after many wanderings throughout the Long Island, had been hiding in a fisherman's hut. Soon the weather spoiled and they ran into heavy seas. It was not till morning that, the mist lifting, they rounded the point of Vaternish and saw the coast of Skye clearly. Then a north-east wind got up and it was rowing all the way until, in the early afternoon, after crossing the broad mouth of Loch Snizort, they landed on the coast of Trotternish, where a burn cuts the beach about two miles north of Kilbride. It had taken the small open 'shallop about nine cubits, wright's measure' — that is, 18ft or so — forty hours to complete the forty miles from Loch Uskavagh. The Prince was in disguise, cutting a curious figure in his linen gown, quilted petticoat, cap and hooded cloak. He was meant to pass as Betty Burke, Miss MacDonald's Irish maid, but it is difficult to see how this tall man, with his big feet, ill at ease in woman's clothes, could have escaped detection had he been apprehended. But the rough and unseasonable weather, which had added so much discomfort to his journeyings, had also served him by preventing the English patrol boats from coming inshore to land search parties. So the little group from Benbecula was safe enough on the beach while Flora went to seek help.

Help came from Monkstadt House. Its owner, Sir Alexander MacDonald of Sleat was away at Fort Augustus on government business. He had enlisted on the Hanoverian side; the Lady Margaret, his wife, was an ardent Jacobite. She was one of the seven beautiful daughters of Susan, Countess of Eglinton and was much loved on the island. Boswell said that she was 'quite adored'. He was told that when she travelled through the island, the people ran in crowds before her and took the stones off the road lest her horse stumbled and she be hurt. He adds that, 'Her husband, Sir Alexander, is also remembered with great regard.' In spite of their different allegiances, the couple seem to have been happy enough. In those times, there was nothing unusual in such a division of loyalties, nor should we suppose that had Sir Alexander been at home, there would have been no help forthcoming for the Prince from Monkstadt House. In the Highlands, the laws of hospitality over-ruled all other considerations. As it was, the Prince had already been succoured by many who did not hold with the Jacobites. Before he landed on Skye, he had been assisted by the tenant of Scalpay, Donald Campbell, whose family had long supported the Whigs. This Donald had also married a Mac-Donald who was a rigid 'loyalist', as Jacobites are sometimes called. Again, the Prince's pilot in the Outer Hebrides as well as on his journey to Skye was one Donald MacLeod, who had risked his life again and again and was eventually captured. In supporting the Prince, he was opposing his clan — as we have seen, its chief, Norman MacLeod of MacLeod had first engaged himself to the Stuarts then, after the Glenfinnan landing, temporised, then gone back on his word.

In the event, the Prince did not stay at Monkstadt: whatever her personal sympathies, Lady Margaret would not have wanted to compromise her husband and, besides, she had quartered upon her one Lieutenant MacLeod of the militia. She appealed to the MacDonald factor, who was known as 'old Kingsburgh' and it was to nearby Kingsburgh House that the Prince was first sent to shelter. From there, he was taken across country to Portree before sailing to Raasay.

In all, Prince Charles Edward spent less than a week on Skye. Yet if Skye can be said to have a tourist industry, it centres on 'Bonnie Prince Charlie' and Flora. Dunvegan may draw all those who bear the old surname; but romantics the world over follow the Stuart trail to the Trotternish peninsula; and Portree, with its own memories of the Prince, makes a good starting point.

The northern half of Skye is divided into three peninsulas. Fanning out from west to east, they are Trotternish, Vaternish and south of Loch Dunvegan, Duirinish. The main road from Portree crossing the south of Trotternish to Snizort at the head of the loch of the same name, then runs north to Uig Bay, in the very heart of the Bonnie Prince Charlie country.

Below the keep on the hill, the bay spreads out in a patchwork of golden arable and green fields. A scattered collection of neat white houses provide homely accommodation. Each has a cheerful cottage garden — something of a rarity in this part of Scotland. In the home-fields there are conical haystacks and tidy piles of peat to fuel winter fires. The hillside is well wooded. Out at sea, fishing boats are setting lobster pots out towards the Ascrib islands where the seals come in the mating season. The car ferry from Harris steams in to the long King Edward's pier, which is named after Queen Victoria's royal son who landed at Uig with Queen Alexandra on a visit to the islands in 1907. It is a quiet, pastoral landscape. Only the dark basalt cliffs which enclose the bay on either side strike a more sombre note. Across Loch Snizort rise the rocky ramparts of Vaternish.

South from Uig, it is less than half a dozen miles to Kingsburgh House. Nowadays, it is a modern mansion standing in its own woods off the Portree road, alongside the deep inlet of Snizort Beag. The old house became Flora MacDonald's home after she married Allan MacDonald in 1750. First they settled at Flodigarry on the north west coast of Trotternish, but in 1755 Allan's father died and he succeeded him as factor to the MacDonald estates. The house went with the job and in the following year, the couple moved to Kingsburgh where their last two children were born, James in 1759 and their second daughter, Frances, in 1766. And there on the 14th of September 1773 they entertained Dr. Johnson and Boswell, who gives us a vivid portrait of his host — and with it, a taste of the quality of life in 18th century Skye. 'Kingsburgh was completely the figure of the gallant Highlander . . . He had his tartan plaid thrown about him, a large blue bonnet with a knot of black ribbon like a cockade, a brown short coat of a kind of duffil (a coarse woollen cloth), a Tartan waistcoat with gold buttons and gold button-holes, a blueish philibeg (kilt), and Tartan hose. He had jet black hair tied behind, and was a large stately man, with a steady sensible countenance.' The picture of his famous wife, who was 51 at the time, is even more tantalising. 'She is a little woman, of a genteel appearance, and uncommonly mild and well-bred.' Both now lie buried in adjoining graves in Kilmuir cemetery.

Travelling north on the way there, we come to Monkstadt, as Mugshot or Mugstot, is now called. The current name is appropriate since it recalls the old Christian settlement which grew up on an island in what was the loch of Chaluim-Chille. The loch was drained in the 1820s, but the remains of the Columban monastery are still there to be explored . . . the ruins of the outer wall, the beehive cells, the tiny primitive chapels . . . among the hay meadows. The landscape itself has changed for we are now in the centre of the 'granary of Skye', as the plain of Kilmuir is aptly called. Then, still travelling north and past Kilmuir itself, the old burial ground stands high above Camus Mor, the 'large bay'. Flora MacDonald's grave is one among many of her kin's, along with the generations of MacArthurs and Nicholsons who were laid to rest on the windswept plateau. A granite slab covers the grave; at its head stands a huge Iona cross and it is believed that a sheet in which the Prince had slept served as her winding-sheet.

The view from Kilmuir cemetery is one of the most beautiful in Skye — to the west, the land slips down to Score Bay, across Loch Snizort, the rugged cliffs of Vaternish cut across the sky and, far out to sea, the dark blue hills of Harris and the long broken line of North Uist and Benbecula melt into cloud and water. Near the churchyard stands an old 'black house', now restored, which serves as the island's Cottage Museum. This most primitive form of Hebridean cottage got its name because its only chimney was a hole in the thatch and the reeking smoke blackened everything within. It makes a perfect setting for the many simple relics of everyday life in Skye long ago.

The little town of Kilmuir itself is the centre of Skye's tweed industry, and from there the road runs north edging Score Bay as far as Duntulm Castle, then cutting off the northern tip of Trotternish, turns south-east to Flodigarry at the foot of the Quiraing massif. The old farm that received the newly-wed Mrs. MacDonald is now a hotel, much enlarged and rebuilt by a branch of the family, the so-called Livingstone MacDonalds. But the original cottage buildings, where Flora's first son, Charles, was born in 1751, is shown to visitors on request. The site itself is charming — with thick woods and bright green grassland where the locals insist that the fairies still dance, and magnificent views over to Flodigarry island. The island is now uninhabited, but it was once the refuge of a holy hermit, St. Turog, who is believed

42

to have given the villagers the two freshwater springs by the shore and the pretty rock pools which serve them as an overflow.

The road to Portree now runs due south along the coast, through Staffin Bay and its several townships, including Staffin itself, which was distinguished by having as its inn the first slate-roofed house to be built on the island; then on, past the much photographed Kilt Rock and the Storr range, also popular with cameramen, and by Loch Fadda, where a monstrous sea-horse once lived, and Loch Leathan. These two Storr lakes, which were once famous for trout, are now the centre of the island's hydroelectric power.

Our Stuart pilgrimage ends at Scorrybeck, with its sheltered landing place, screened off by a small headland. It was there at McNicol's Rock that Prince Charles Edward landed and went into hiding on his return from Raasay. At Portree, we see the Prince and Flora together for the last time, in the old thatched inn over the harbour where the Royal Hotel now stands. The Stuarts seldom paid their debts, so it is pleasant to recall that on this occasion Prince Charlie did so — handing Flora back a half-crown that he had borrowed, as he parted from her. He reached the mainland safely and after further adventures there was taken off by the French ship, L'Heureux, sailing from Borrodale. It was the 19th of September 1747 and he had been fourteen months in Scotland; he was never to see his ancestral land again. By then Flora, too, had left Skye, for an exile which was to last several years.

The boatmen who had brought the Prince over from the Long Island had been allowed to return to South Uist. They were apprehended, questioned and under threat of torture, told their story. A week or so after leaving the Prince at Portree, Flora was arrested at her mother's home in Armadale. From Skye, she was taken to Leith in the sloop, Furness, under the command of the notoriously brutal Captain Ferguson. However, General Campbell was also on board and, at his instance, Miss MacDonald

43

was treated courteously. While the Furness lay at anchor in Leith, the ladies of Edinburgh came out in their carriages to visit Flora and made much of her. And the same welcome awaited her when she arrived in London. She became the talk of the town, money was collected to provide her with comforts, society called and it is said that the Prince of Wales himself came to visit her. She was never put on trial and was released the following year in the general amnesty under the Act of Indemnity of 1747. After a lengthy stay in Edinburgh, where she was feted, she returned to Skye in 1750. Prince Charles Edward died in 1788. He is commemorated in the fine Jacobite poem, known in translation as 'The White Cockade':

> 'Ancient Scotland! A tale of woe
> Every sea-wave breaking brings,
> That thy royal heir is now in Rome
> Earthed in chest of polished boards'

Flora's finest epitaph was written by Doctor Johnson. It runs: 'A name that will be mentioned in history, and if courage and fidelity be virtues, mentioned with honour.'

Car Excursions

'Bonnie Prince Charlie' country has, so to speak, two centres — Uig and Portree.

From **Uig**, the 855 running north enters the plain of Kilmuir through a series of steep hairpin bends. At the top of the hill drive straight on, ignoring the right-hand turn for Staffin, as far as Linicro. Past the village, a small side road leads towards the coast to Monkstadt. To the south lies Kilbride Point and the Bay, and to the north, the reclaimed marsh of Challuim-Chille, with its Columban ruins. Carry on north through Bala-gown to the burial ground of Kilmuir above the shores of Camus Mor (the Great Bay). Past Kilmuir, the road then reaches Score Bay, a total distance of under 10 miles.

Turning south from Uig, the 856, the same road as for Dunvegan, leads past Hinnisdal Bridge along the shores of Loch Snizort. Just about two miles from the bridge a side road branches off to the right to Kinsburgh House, while the 856 runs on to the villages of Romesdal and Kensaleyre (past Snizort Church), where it joins the 850 to Portree (east) and Dunvegan (south west).

As we have already seen, there are a number of ways of reaching **Flodigarry**. Travellers from Portree have in the 855 one of the best as well as the most spectacular roads in the island. North, then, along the 855, past the hydro-electric lochs Fadda and Leathan, and five miles further on, a first sight of the Old Man as the roads run under the Storr. Continue over the Lealt river to Loch Mealt and Staffin. There, the road turns inland to follow the contours of Staffin Bay, then runs almost due north again alongside the Quiraing range to Flodigarry.

CROFT AT LUIB

FLORA McDONALD MONUMENT
SKYE

'I had desired to visit the Hebrides'

When Dr. Johnson and James Boswell sailed in to Portree on the 12th of September 1773, the capital of Skye had changed very little in the nearly thirty years that had elapsed since Prince Charles Edward had stopped there briefly on his way back to France and his final exile in Italy. There was a church where the travellers heard the office, read in Gaelic by their friend, Donald MacQueen. There was the inn where they entertained more friends and which Boswell described as 'tolerable'. Otherwise, Portree had nothing but a huddle of 'black houses' by the bank of the loch, the old gaol on the hillside and the gallows on the 'Lump', the name given to the craggy, wooded bluff over the harbour, where the last hanging on Skye took place in 1742. Portree had no curiosities to offer them, but the harbour was another matter . . .

'The port is made by an inlet of the sea, deep and narrow', wrote Dr. Johnson, 'where a ship was waiting to dispeople Skye, by carrying the natives to America'. A party was made up to visit her, and while Dr. Johnson remained in the boat discoursing with Mr. MacQueen, Boswell who was ever avid of novelties, went aboard. The ship was called the Nestor. 'She was a verry pretty vessel, and, as we were told, the largest in the Clyde. Mr. Harrisson, the captain, shewed her to us. The cabin was commodious, and even elegant. There was a little library, finely bound.' A heartless comment, this, when not only individual families, but whole neighbourhoods were being hounded from their homes. A few days later, however, Boswell was moved to pity when, over on the west coast, by Ulinish, he came across another boatload of emigrants. 'In the morning I walked out, and saw a ship, the Margaret of Clyde, pass by with a number of emigrants on board. It was a melancholy sight', he wrote.

It is a common mistake to blame emigration on the 19th century Clearances, when men were displaced to make room for sheep. But the slow depopulation of the Islands had been going on for two hundred years at least before sheep-farming was put on to an economic basis, and Dr. Johnson was quick to see why. Wherever they went, Johnson and Boswell heard emigration discussed and deplored and Johnson pitied the plight of the poor people and promptly took their masters to task, perhaps unfairly. 'Some method to stop this epidemick desire of wandering deserves to be sought with great diligence. In more fruitful countries, the removal of one only makes room for the succession of another: but in the Hebrides, the loss of an inhabitant leaves a lasting vacuity; for nobody born in any other part of the world will choose this country for residence, and an island once depopulated will remain a desert.' He goes on to state bluntly: 'that the immediate cause for their desertion must be imputed to their landlords, may be reasonably concluded, because some lairds of more prudence and less rapacity have kept their vassals undiminished. From Raasa only one man has been seduced, and at Col there was no wish to go away.' As though to illustrate the point, he speaks of Sir Alexander MacDonald who was reputed to be unnerved on sea-journeys. '*He* is frightened at sea; and his tenants are frightened when he comes to land.' He remained firm in his opinion that 'a rapacious chief would make a wilderness of his estate.'

Good landlords, however, were often hard put to provide a livelihood for their tenants and it was not unusual for the gentry themselves to seek better fortune overseas. Several of Dr. Johnson's hosts in Skye were thinking of emigrating; a year after they entertained him, the MacDonalds left for America, where they spent 25 years farming. With two of their sons they settled in

North Carolina, near Campbelltown (now Fayetteville) where it is estimated that about 10,000 Highlanders had already preceded them.

The policy of enclosing land — already common practice in Tudor times — was now firmly rooted in England and was spreading north. It may have aggravated emigration but it was not altogether to blame for the progressive depopulation of the Highlands and Islands. The problem was not in fact man-made: where the soil is too poor to sustain those working on it, sooner or later they will leave to try their luck elsewhere. Besides, the agricultural system which operated in 18th century Skye made matters worse. The holdings — or crofts, for the word does not denote the dwelling-house alone — were small, sometimes no more than one or two acres and never exceeding 100. They were let out annually by the laird, or by his agents, the tacksmen, to a group of farmers who worked the land in common and shared the profits on the 'run-rig' system. Each man then took the benefits of the 'rig', or ridge assigned to him. The rigs themselves were re-allocated after the harvest so that everyone had his turn at the best and the poorest land. The land was further sub-divided into outfields representing about three quarters of the total acreage, and individual in-fields which provided each tenant with his own small parcel of land, often hardly more than a cabbage patch. What manure there was was kept for the in-fields but, even so, the crofter could not keep all his home produce, for part of the rent was paid in kind and this included vegetables for the manor house. Outfields, which were farmed in common, were cropped to exhaustion over several years, then allowed to revert to moorland, which provided rough pasturage for the cattle. The disadvantages of this type of community farming were many: the precarious annual tenancies discouraged improvements, the cultivation of the outfields on a uniform plan did not allow for the individual nature of the soil and the extent of the total acreage was generally far too small to support the number of tenants who depended on it. In these conditions, neither master nor man was tempted to explore modern methods of cultivation or invest in up-to-date machinery.

Many of the farm implements which are now on display in folk museums were still in use not so long ago. Middle-aged men in Skye have used the old 'crooked spade' which Dr. Johnson saw and described, noting how heavy and incommodious it seemed to him. 'It has a narrow blade of iron fixed to a long and heavy piece of wood, which must have, about a foot and a half above the iron, a knee or flexure with the angle downwards. When the farmer encounters a stone which is the great impediment of his operations, he drives the blade under it, and bringing the knee or angle to the ground, has in the long handle a very forcible level.' A variant of the crooked spade was the 'cas-chrom', a sort of wooden foot-plough, and there were hoes, scythes and the local sickle, the 'corran'. For the heaviest tasks, enormous wooden ploughs were dragged by teams of oxen, and the beasts were so meagre that it took eight to make up a team. Even so, it was a day's work to scratch up half-an-acre.

The chief crop was barley, which was the staple food; oats ('A grain, which in England is given to horses, but in Scotland supports the people' runs the famous description in Dr. Johnson's Dictionary) went to make Scottish ale as well as the ubiquitous scones. Potatoes which were feeding the population of Ireland were grown only in the in-field as a delicacy for the laird's table. In Dr. Johnson's day, the rotation of crops, which had radically altered the English countryside and revolutionised its agrarian economy, was still unpractised in Scotland. As long as the run-rig system persisted, it was not practicable to cultivate more than one crop in the open fields.

The root crops, introduced in England under George the Second and George the Third by such great innovators as 'Turnip' Townsend and Coke of Norfolk, had so much improved the cattle's winter feed that the weight of English steers was said to have doubled in the course of the 18th century. In the Highlands, however, all but the cattle kept for breeding were still slaughtered before the winter set in, and the meat salted down, as it had been since medieval times. The remaining beasts were brought in, often sharing the dwelling-house with its human inhabitants.

There, they nearly starved on their winter rations of straw and boiled chaff and were further weakened by the horrid practice of bleeding — drawing fresh blood to mix and enrich the oat-cakes. When the spring came, the cattle were led back to the rough moorland pastures — the operation was called 'lifting' and the unfortunate beasts were so much impaired by the long winter's starvation diet that the term was sadly descriptive. Livestock is still one of the island's main resources; since the last war, as many as 40,000 head of cattle have been exported annually. Although modern grazing has improved their condition beyond compare, the cattle are still sold on the hoof to be fattened for the market on the rich grass of the Lowlands and, across the border, in lush English meadows.

Today's cattle markets in Skye — held twice a year at Portree — attract farmers from all over Britain; a dwindling number of those who attend them still remember the cattle droves of the old days, when man and beast travelled some 200 miles to market. They went by water from Kylerhea to Glenelg, then on foot right across Scotland to the famous Falkirk Tryst, north of Edinburgh, near the Firth of Forth. When Thomas Pennant returned to Skye in 1772, he described the operation as he saw it that summer. 'The horned cattle of Ski are swam over, at the narrow passage of Kul-ri, at low water; six, eight or twelve are passed over at a time, tied with rope, fastened from the horn of one to its tail, and so to the next; the first is fastened to a boat, and thus are conveyed to the opposite shore. This is the great pass into the island, but is destitute even of a horse-ferry.'

The great days of sheep farming, made possible by the controversial Highland Clearances, were yet to come, but the crofters all kept a few sheep as well as goats. The wool went to make their homespun clothes, and both animals provided milk. As Dr. Johnson was told: 'a single meal of a goat is about a quart, and of a sheep, a pint', and the sheep's milk which was 'very liberal of curd' was occasionally made into small cheeses.

The island's simple economy was further varied by fishing and by the profitable kelp industry. A special sort of sea-weed was cut and burnt for its ashes which were used in the manufacture of glass. In the 18th century, ships called regularly at the islands to collect cargoes of kelp-ash. The work was done chiefly by women and children and in the middle of the century, they earned two or three pounds during the season. But the trade died out when the glass industry came to dispense with ash and the maritime farms were deprived of this welcome addition to their slender incomes. On the other hand, rather more sea-weed was available for manuring the croftlands.

There was, of course, plenty of fish, including both eels and trout and, according to some authorities, so much salmon that it was despised by the gentry and left to the common folk. 'The meanest servants, who are not on board wages, will not make a meal upon salmon, if they can get anything else to eat', Edward Burt was writing in 1726. We hear too of 'cuddy' or gudgeon which provided the crofters with a fresh meal as well as with lamp oil in such abundance that they were able to sell the excess. Towards the end of the century, the authorities began to consider that sea fishing might prove the salvation of the Highlands. The seas of the West Coast teemed with fish — with ling and cod and haddock, flat fish and mackerel and great shoals of herring which came down the coast in June and stocked the Minch, the sea-lochs and the Hebridean waters. The latter were highly prized by Thomas Pennant who wrote of 'their superiority in goodness over those of the South: they were not larger, but as they had not wasted themselves by being in roe, their backs and the part next to the tail were double the thickness of the others, and the meat rich beyond expression'. The herring catch was colossal — each vessel taking up to a hundred barrels in a single night — but most of it was made by the great Dutch herring-busses which came in powerful fleets to fish the deep waters, while the British vessels operated along the coast. The Clyde was the centre of the industry, drying and salting the fish for export. But all this profitable activity largely bypassed the Highlanders — they were too poor to own trawlers and because of the salt tax, they could not afford to preserve what fish they caught. Some effort was made on their behalf by the newly-founded Society for the Encouragement of the British Fisheries, as well as by private landowners. The Society established Ullapool as a fishing village in 1788 and founded Tobermory on the Isle of Mull in the same year. Stornoway on the Isle of Lewis was developed by the Earl of Seaforth and, although it had no pier, sheltered a small British fleet of about two dozen decked vessels. After the '45, the Duke of Argyll rebuilt the castle of Inverary and its lovely little town as a herring-port. It stands on Loch Fyne, south of Oban, but it was never very successful although its romantic setting was already attracting travellers in the 18th century. On Skye itself, Stein in Vaternish was purpose-built to encourage local fisheries, but the project failed and it remains a pretty village by the sea shore with pleasure boats on the beach. Fishing is now ably assisted by Government subsidies and much is made of the lobsters, crabs, prawns and even oysters in which the Hebrides abound. But unreliable weather and the dangerous coast are against its ever becoming a major and sufficient source of revenue. 'If it were always practicable to fish, the islands could never be in much danger of famine; but unhappily in the winter, when other provisions fail, the seas are commonly too rough for nets, or boats' as Dr. Johnson wrote. After the Highland clearances, many of the evicted crofters were resettled along the shore in the hope that they would take to fishing for a livelihood. When this experiment, and subsequent ones, failed, the alleged laziness of the Hebridean was blamed:

'Oh that the peats would cut themselves,
The fish slump on the shore,
And that we all in bed might lie
For aye and evermore'

Even today, round the villages of Waterloo, Scullamus, Breakish, Harrapool, the sight of roofless cottages and upturned boats rotting on the shore are witness to the landsman's reluctance to take to the sea in a hopeless fight against the elements.

These and many other instances of the island's tenuous economy were noted for inclusion in 'A Journey to the Western Islands . . .' and the 'Journal of a Tour of the Hebrides' respectively, by Dr. Johnson and by James Boswell as they traced their irregular course through Skye. As was the custom of the times, they travelled from place to place, staying with friends and acquaintances. The company of the compiler of the great 'Dictionary' was much sought after; everyone wanted to meet the author of the 'Rambler' whose each number had sold out fast on the streets of Edinburgh. The Scots are a learned as well as a hospitable people; and for any who might have hesitated to open their doors to the son of a Lichfield bookseller, the presence of James Boswell, son and heir of Lord Auchinleck, acted as a guarantee. A letter from 'his most obedient and most humble servant' Lord Elibank is token of the eagerness with which Dr. Johnson was received by the great. It reads: 'I was to have kissed your hands at Edinburgh, the moment I heard of you; but you was gone. I hope my friend Boswell will inform me of your motions. It will be cruel to deprive me an instant of the honour of attending you. As I value you more than any King in Christendom, I will perform that duty with infinitely greater alacrity than any courtier.'

Invitations came in plenty, but the travellers had to rely on their would-be hosts for transport, by sea as well as by land, when guides and horses had to be found. As a result, there were delays and false starts, and the pattern of their journeyings through Skye and the neighbouring islands was highly erratic.

We met them first on the beach at Armadale, where they landed after spending a wretched night at an inn in Glenelg. Rather than take the bed offered them which 'a man as black as a Cyclops from the forge' had given up to the gentry, they procured some hay and lay on it, Johnson in his riding coat while Boswell, having unpacked his sheets, 'lay in linen like a gentleman.' As to food, 'of the provisions, the negative catalogue was very copious. Here was no meat, no bread, no eggs, no wine'. They had brought bread with them, and received a present of rum and sugar when their guide's master heard of their arrival. That was on the 1st of September (1773); and the next day, their first in Skye, they reposed in comfort under the roof of Sir Alexander MacDonald, and from then on were assured of a good bed every night of their stay in the island, though they often travelled a circuitous route to reach it. As Johnson said, 'a very few miles require several hours.'

A few days later, they were at Coire Chatachan as guests of Mr. MacKinnon. The ruins of the house are still there. Johnson described it as 'very pleasantly situated between two brooks, with one of the highest hills on the island behind it,' adding in a much-quoted phrase, 'the hill behind the house we did not climb'. The weather was bad, the climb was steep and the 'numerous and elegant company' that had foregathered at Mr. MacKinnon's tempted them to stay indoors. But it is a pity to miss the view from the top of the Fairy Hill, 'An Sidhean', with its wide prospect of the Red Hills, Strath Sworddale and, a little further down the road to Elgol, the loch of Kilchrist, with its creeper-covered church and ancient cemetery. At Coire Chatachan, another invitation came to visit Raasay, but the continuous bad weather detained them and Boswell began to feel that the hospitable house had become a prison.

Every holiday-maker knows the sad sound of the rain on the window-pane and feels the dullness that descends when a grey mist blots out yesterday's brilliant landscape, as it so often does in Scotland. But in the 18th century a prolonged downpour had the serious disadvantage of putting a stop to all travelling. The roads became impassable, horses slithered, what wheeled traffic there was bogged down. In England, the passing of the Turnpike Act of 1751 — the last in a very long series of such Acts since the days of Queen Anne — had brought about an enormous improvement in the roads which were now crowded with a variety of elegant carriages, as well as the heavy stage-coaches. Travelling from Edinburgh to Aberdeen, Dr. Johnson and Boswell had made use of post-chaises, which were much faster than the public stage-coaches, though 'shaying', as it was called, was expensive. In the Highlands, however, they had taken to riding on horseback since there were neither roads nor posting-inns at which to get fresh relays of horses. It had taken them a full and hard day's riding to get from Armadale to Coire Chatachan. 'In the islands there are no roads, nor any marks by which a stranger can find his way. The horseman has always at his side a native of the place who, by pursuing game, or tending cattle, or being often employed in messages or conduct, has learned when the ridge of the hill has breadth sufficient to allow a horse and his rider a passage and where the bog or moss is hard enough to bear them. The bogs are avoided as toilsome at least, if not unsafe, and therefore the journey is made generally from precipice to precipice . . . The Highlander walks carefully before, and the horse, accustomed to the ground, follows him with little deviation. Sometimes the hill is too steep for the horseman to keep his seat, and sometimes the moss is too tremulous to bear the double weight of horse and man. The rider then dismounts, and all shift as they can.' The modern motorist now drives quietly along the excellent coast road, oblivious of these arduous conditions, which are familiar only to climbers in the wildest parts of Skye. But if ramblers bore in mind what the Doctor had to say about bogs, there would be fewer expensive misadventures on Skye.

It was on horseback again that Johnson and Boswell rode down to the coast to take passage to Raasay, in a strong boat built in Norway, which had been sent over by their host, MacLeod of Raasay. This considerable landlord owned, besides Raasay, the outlying islands of Rona and Fladday, as well as extensive acreage in Skye itself. He owed allegiance to MacLeod of Dunvegan and was in alliance with MacDonald as well. The sea was rough, but the crossing was a merry one: with four stout oarsmen, they crossed along Scalpay the boat riding the waves well. The crew sang a ballad in Gaelic and the pilot, Mr. Malcolm MacLeod joined in the chorus. He was 62 at the time, but Boswell thought him a striking figure — bare-kneed in full Highland rig of tartan hose, purple kilt, a black waistcoat and a large blue bonnet topping his bushy wig. The seas grew heavier as they left the shelter of Scalpay to cross the sound. Dr. Johnson, sitting high in the stern 'like a magnificent triton' lost a pair of spurs, washed overboard. It was their only misadventure and soon they came into the calmer waters of Raasay Bay where a large party, led by Raasay himself, had come down to meet them.

Raasay is less than fifteen miles long and under four miles across. It has often been described as a small replica of Skye, formed of the same geological elements and offering the same scenery in miniature. Here are rocks, and heath and braes where the blackface sheep nibble the short, salty grass; here is the blue skyline broken by the crests of high hills, here are cornlands where the reapers were singing on that September day when Johnson and Boswell disembarked. The island's rocky formation dictates the variety of its landscape — in the north, gneiss and Torridonian sandstone; in the south, sandstone of the Jurassic period, lime, shale and ironstone. Iron was much mined on Raasay until the First World War — now there remains only a disused opencast working hard by the landing stage. The island is crowned by a high plateau of basalt — Dun Can or Raasay's Cap as the sailors call this landmark which rises to nearly 1,500 ft in a small-scale version of MacLeod's Tables. Though the path is stony, the ascent of Dun Can is an easy climb, by gradual stages to the top. From the summit there is a beautiful view over the mainland and the Outer Isles, which include off the north-west coast, the tiny islands of Fladday and Eilean Tighe. Both can be reached at low tide by the causeway that runs at the foot of the cliffs. Due north, across a narrow kyle, Raasay is extended by another rocky island, South Rona. All these islands are uninhabited, and if we are to believe Dr. Johnson who said that Rona grazed 160 head of cattle under the supervision of a solitary herdsman, have been so for a very long time. Rona, however, has a small harbour as well as a lighthouse, and for pilgrims of antiquities, the ruins of a little Celtic chapel. In the old days, Rona was a notorious haunt of pirates and smugglers. Illicit distillers of 'moonshine' whisky found it a safe hideaway, and for all we know, still do.

Like Skye again, Raasay has its ruined castles, of which the most interesting and picturesque is Brochel, overlooking a fine bay in the east. It is built on two levels over a volcanic substructure. Boswell visited it and found there a curiosity which he describes delicately as 'a certain accommodation rarely to be found at the modern houses in Scotland', including Raasay itself. Dr. Johnson's comment on his host's lack of lavatories was less delicate: 'You take very good care of one end of man, but not of the other.'

For me, by far the most attractive thing about Raasay is Raasay House itself. It was rebuilt in 1773 when Dr. Johnson and Boswell stayed there, and is in consequence that rare thing in the Highlands — a pretty, perfect Georgian home. Standing on a slope, backed by a semi-circle of woods, it overlooks a greensward, landscaped by clumps of deciduous trees, which sweeps down to the waters of the bay. It is no stately mansion, but a goodly house, standing four-square to the sea, in all its simple and solid Georgian grace. Though less impressed than we are by an architecture which to them was commonplace, both Johnson and Boswell were well pleased with it. Boswell wrote: 'We saw before us a beautiful bay, well defended by a rocky coast; a good family mansion; a fine verdure about it, — with a considerable number of trees, — and beyond it hills and mountains in gradations of wildness.'

Now a sad fate has overtaken the old Raasay home. A few years ago it was bought by a 'southron' from England's home counties. Wishing neither to take up residence nor to relinquish his rights — which are said incidentally to include all the island's fishing as well as certain mineral concessions — this absentee landlord is leaving the house to look after itself, unprotected from the elements and at the mercy of vandals. Now its windows are broken, the glass in the conservatory is shattered, sea damp creeps up (is the Indian bed which welcomed Dr. Johnson to its soft sheets still standing?), weeds have invaded the flower garden and the trees are fallen in the old orchard with its crumbling walls. Where now are the strawberry beds which Boswell celebrated? Local bodies are active and the authorities are taking a hand, but litigation is cumbersone and the law is slow. It is said that in the 400 years that the MacLeods were in possession, they held Raasay intact, neither adding nor losing an acre of their territory. It will not take 10 years to destroy Raasay House, for the weather is already withering it away.

The rainfall in Raasay is high — even for the Highlands, and bad weather, 'beating billows and howling storm', again forced Dr. Johnson and Boswell to extend their stay. During their last days on the island, they were able to make one more sortie — to a ruined chapel in the grounds. This small relic from the origins of Christianity in the Hebrides is dedicated to St. Moluag of Lismore, an Irish contemporary of St. Columba who carried the gospels to the Picts of the northern lands. On the shore nearby, Boswell knelt in prayer before a Celtic cross of curious design. Among the island's several antiquities, both the chapel and the cross still attract visitors.

The sun shone again, and the travellers returned to the mainland to take up the invitation which had come from the chief of the clan, The MacLeod of MacLeod himself, to visit him at Dunvegan. While their companion sailed to Sconser — as we do today — they took the overland route via Portree and the hospitality of Flora MacDonald at Kingsburgh. Here Dr. Johnson lay in the bed where Prince Charles Edward had rested in 1746. Boswell wrote: 'To see Dr. Johnson lying in that bed, in the isle of Skye, in the house of Miss Flora MacDonald, struck me with such a group of ideas as it is not easy for words to describe, as they passed through the mind'. It was while they were staying at Kingsburgh that he composed a full account of the Prince's flight through the islands and learnt of the part that his recent host had played in the adventure. He was told how the Prince had been brought from Portree to Raasay in a small boat which had been carried overland from Loch Fada to a safe harbour near the town, then rowed overnight to Raasay and hidden there in a shepherd's hut. He was told, no doubt by Flora herself, that the Raasay Mac-Leods, unlike their chief, had remained faithful to the Stuarts and of the terrible retribution which had come to the island. It was the very Malcolm MacLeod who had so merrily piloted them over to Raasay only five days ago, who had led a 100 men

58

from Raasay to Drumossie Moor. From the battlefield not more than 14 returned. Yet he and his overlord had been ready once again to shelter their Prince. The Prince escaped but Raasay paid heavily for its loyalty. Shortly after Culloden, a party of Hanoverian troops landed there and burned down every house in the island — three hundred of them according to contemporary accounts.

Now, in 1773, all this was history. Factional feeling had died out, and Dr. Johnson and Boswell had no compunction in leaving the hospitality of the MacDonalds to enjoy that of Dunvegan Castle. The weather had worsened again and they made part of the journey by boat to the shores of Loch Greshornish, not far from the pleasant hamlet of Edinbain from where the road now strikes west to the Fairy Bridge. But they rode south to Dunvegan, through the great stretches of machair and purple moorland which characterises this northern reach of Skye, with its queer table mountains, crested cliffs, rocky pinnacles and distant views of the sugar-cone mountains of Harris.

They were now nearing the end of their Highland trip; soon they would be on their way south and homewards, making a final detour to visit the Isle of Mull. Their last days in Skye were busy: at Dunvegan, there was the castle and its many antiquities to explore and record, and its neighbourhood to visit. MacLeod's hospitality was lavish, 'so elegant in style' that Dr. Johnson who had had a bad fall riding over the moor and had taken cold as well became quite 'joyous' and announced, 'Boswell, we came in at the wrong end of the island' — a sentiment modern tourists may well endorse. He slept in Rorie Mor's bedchamber and like the great Roderick himself was lulled to sleep by the sound of the cascade. In bed he wore a fine flannel nightcap which Miss MacLeod had made him when it was found the he had none by him. Next morning, they were shown other relics of Rorie's day — they looked at his famous horn, 'a large cow's horn, with the mouth of it ornamented with silver curiously carved. It holds rather more than a bottle and a half. Every Laird of MacLeod, it is said, must as a proof of his manhood, drink it off full of claret, without laying it down.' When the rain stopped, they examined the garden and saw Rorie's cascade close to. Back in the castle, they admired the armoury and were duly impressed by his bow 'which hardly any man can now bend' and by his claymore, the ancient sword of 'prodigious size' which was yielded with both hands.

During these final days, they made time for several excursions. They visited Ulinish, where they admired the garden and fine trees of Ulinish House. Boswell borrowed a rod to go fishing and caught cuddy. In Bracadale, they noted the first snows on the Cuillins. But it seems they missed one of the island's finest sights — the famous Coral Beach which lies on Loch Dunvegan's northern shore. A track runs from the castle for about four miles over the springy turf, then a breach in the cliffs leads down to the beach. I failed to establish whether it were true coral or, as some say, a form of fossilized seaweed, but it shines pure white between the black basalt cliffs and the green sea and when the sun is out, there are only the seals at play to remind one that these are not the West Indies, but the Hebrides.

Next our travellers rode south by Loch Harport and across the north of the Minginish peninsula to stay with a Colonel MacLeod of the Dutch service at Talisker. Both were impressed, a little awed perhaps, by the surroundings and wild seascape. Dr. Johnson: 'It is situated very near the sea, but upon a coast where no vessel lands but when it is driven by a tempest on the rocks. Towards the land are lofty hills streaming with water-falls'. And Boswell: 'Before it is a wide expanse of sea, on each hand of which are immense rocks; the billows break with prodigious force and noise on the coast of Talisker'. He makes no mention of the 900 ft drop of basalt cliff at Talisker Head, but he did count the water-falls — 15 of them within a quarter of a mile of the house — and drank the water of Cuchullin's Well which he found 'admirable'. Today all these waters go to the making of the famous malt whisky from the Talisker Distillery and, with the peat used to dry the grain, lend it its distinctive flavour. Visitors are welcomed to the distillery.

Fortified by a dram or two, they can then make their way from Carbost down to the sands of Talisker Bay or going west to the pretty village of Fiskavaig, end the day's outing watching the sun set in splendour over the sea. Anglers will take the hill track to the head of Loch Eynort and the salmon river, Drynoch, and mountaineers go south to Glenbrittle, the headquarters of the southern Cuillins, or back along the river to Sligachan.

Dr. Johnson and Boswell went south to Sleat to wait for a fair wind for their journey to Mull, but it is at Dunvegan that we should leave them to give place to another of the castle's famous guests, Sir Walter Scott.

Car Excursions

Some highlights of Johnson's visit to Skye:

Coire Chatachan: The trip is best made from Broadford, along the 881 to Elgol. There is nothing much left of MacKinnon's house, whose ruins are of interest to dedicated Johnsonians only. But almost at once on leaving Broadford the shapely horseshoe of the Red Cuillin springs into view, dominated by the two summits of Benn Dearg and Benn na Caillich. Past Coire Chatachan, the road runs through Strath Swarddale along the shores of Loch Kilchrist on to Kilbride and Torrin. It then encircles the head of Loch Slapin amid the lovely scenery of Blaven and Clach Glas.

Talisker: Take the 863 from Sligachan along Glen Drynoch and the river which gives its name to the town by the head of Loch Harport. Just short of the town, cross the river bridge on to a good secondary road which branches off south of the loch (west) to Carbost and the Talisker Distillery. The B8009 then runs along the south shore of the loch to end up at Fiskavaig. From Carbost, another road running west crosses the waterfall and leads across the peninsula to the town of Talisker. From there a footpath takes one down to the sands of the bay and to Talisker Point. Carbost is also the starting point for a visit

61

Loch Coruisk

Elgol

Dunvegan Castle

Coral Beach, Loch Dunvegan

to Loch Eynort — over the waterfall carry on west as for Talisker, and after a mile take the road due south to the head of the loch.

Raasay: Though the ferry from Sconser takes cars, Raasay is perhaps best visited on foot or by hiring a bicycle locally. The island's chief village is Inverarish, with a good shop and the Creachan Cottage Youth Hostel nearby. A reasonably well surfaced secondary road starts near Ayre Point in the south and runs along the west coast past the village along to Raasay House, then north to Holoman where it zig-zags inland and carries on to Brochel and the castle on the east coast facing the mainland. From Brochel, a coastal track along the steep cliffs — unsuitable for cars — completes the circuit of the island. In its northern section, there are plenty of footpaths which, tides permitting, lead on to Fladday across the kyle and to Eilean Tighe.

The ascent of Dun Can is perhaps best left to experienced climbers for there are deep fissures in the vicinity, but the forest walks and charming paths under the fuschia hedges on the low-lying hills are there for less ambitious walkers.

Crossings are made from Sconser and Loch Sligachan — check the times (which vary considerably) locally. Motor boats can also be had for hire. All water traffic avoids the Narrows of Raasay — the shortest crossing as the crow flies — because of the dangerous tidal races.

OLD MAN OF STORR
SKYE

The Heart is Highland

In 1976 Scotland welcomed over one million tourists for the first time in its recorded history. The Scottish Tourist Board in announcing the figures did not break them down, so we do not know for a certainty how many of the country's visitors went to the Highlands and the Hebrides. But it is a fair guess that sooner or later a goodly proportion took 'the road to the isles'.

The way so far largely unexplored was first charted by Sir Walter Scott when, in the summer of 1814, he took a cruise and, by way of Aberdeen and the Orkneys, sailed into Loch Dunvegan on the morning of the 23rd of August and woke beneath the old castle's walls. One result of this excursion was his epic poem, 'The Lord of the Isles'.

By the first decade of the nineteenth century, relations between the Scottish Lowlands and England were frequent and friendly. Once Edinburgh's New Town, with its graceful Georgian squares, had been built below the Castle, bypassing the narrow medieval wynds that ran off the High Street and the Cowgate, the Scottish capital became the true metropolis of the north and began to rival even London in sophistication. By 1810, a few adventurous travellers had pushed as far as Loch Lomond and even Ben Nevis, but the trickle became a flood when in that year 'The Lady of the Lake' was published. The poem is set around Loch Katrine beneath the mighty shadow of Ben Lomond; the first edition of about 2,000 copies sold out on publication and within a few months, more than 20,000 had left the presses. Walter Scott was famous; and so were the Trossachs. Visitors hurried there in their hundreds and the revenue from the duty on post-horses rose steadily from that date. By the time the 'Lord of the Isles' appeared, Walter Scott had found a rival on the literary scene in his fellow Scotsman, George Gordon, Lord Byron, yet there is no doubt that the two volumes taken in conjunction introduced a whole generation to the magnificent scenery of the Highlands and fathered its tourist trade.

Walter Scott was himself a Lowlander, born in Edinburgh and brought up in the Border country, where he was sent to recover from an early attack of infantile paralysis. Growing up in his grandfather's home in Sandyknowe, the little boy fell in love — a love that was to last his lifetime — with the charm of these uplands between the rivers Yarrow and Tweed, with the Cheviot hills in the blue distance across the border. In the neighbourhood stood the great ruined abbeys at Melrose and Jedburgh. He explored them and from them learnt much of his country's tempestuous history, to which the many solitary peel towers against the skyline attested. He learnt more from the old ballads and legends that the countryfolk sang to him as they sat by the fireside on long winter evenings or, in summer, tended their flocks on the hillside.

Walter Scott's lameness remained with him throughout his life: it turned him into the great poet and novelist he became rather than the soldier he had wanted to be. But his lameness did not impede his forays into the countryside — he became an excellent horseman and rode far afield in search of the background against which the fierce feuds of the clans, the passionate action of the Covenanters and the romantic attempts of the Stuarts to regain the throne had been fought out. In his many novels of 'old, unhappy, far-off things and battles long ago', it is the scenery at least as much as the cast that we remember, travel to visit and return to enjoy.

Readers of the Hebridean diaries of Dr. Johnson and James Boswell know how few references they contain to the landscape: both were endlessly curious about the social customs, manners and institutions and assiduous in recording every detail of Skye's historic past, but for its natural heritage they cared nothing. In this they were of their age. 'Caledonia, stern and wild' was not for the 18th century; until the coming of England's Lake Poets and of Walter Scott, nature was ignored. Snowy mountain peaks, dark lochs and sunlit glens, shaggy forest, wild heath and empty moorland were then no more than milestones, and sometimes weary obstacles, to the traveller on his way to the fine claret and civilized conversation which was his journey's goal. In the grounds of its stately homes, the 18th century gentleman would construct an ornamental lake or a cascade to flow from a shell-lined grotto dedicated to Neptune surrounded by his stucco Tritons, but the shining waterfall down the mountainside had no appeal, when nature to be admired must be curbed and corseted.

Now the Age of Enlightenment was drawing to a close, romance was taking over from reason and it was with a poet's eye that Walter Scott was able to view Skye, naked and unadorned.

One of the sights to impress him most was the famous Spar Cave: on the east coast of Strathaird — the peninsula which thrusts out to sea between Loch Scavaig and Loch Slapin — it is best reached by motor-boat from the little town of Glanaskille. Writing in his Journal, Walter Scott describes it thus: 'The roof, floor and walls seem as if they were sheeted with marble, partly smooth, partly rough with fretwork and rustic ornaments, and partly seeming to be wrought into statuary. The floor might be fancifully compared to a sheet of water which, while it rushed whitening and foaming down a declivity, had been suddenly arrested and consolidated by the spell of an enchanter. The cave opens into a splendid gallery, adorned with the most dazzling crystallisations, and finally descends with rapidity to the brink of a pool of the most limpid water. There opens beyond this pool a portal arch, formed by two columns of white spar, with beautiful chasings upon the sides. The groups of combined figures projecting, or embossed, by which the pool is surrounded, are exquisitely elegant and fanciful. A statuary might catch beautiful hints from the singular and romantic disposition of these stalactites.'

Visitors to Scott's 'enchanted cell' have done it much mischief, and it is little consolation to read that in the year 1814, vandals were already at work. 'Many of those fine groups have been injured by the senseless rage of appropriation of recent tourists', he writes.

Higher up the coast, within an easy drive, lies the Piper's Cave at Harlosh, so-called because it is one of several by which legend says that the first MacCrimmon piper, playing his pipes and with his small terrier at his heels, returned to fairyland (see page 71). Dr. Johnson put to sea with Boswell to visit Harlosh as well as the Archway cave at Greep. 'The sea was smooth. We never left the shore, and came without any disaster to the cavern, which we found rugged and misshapen, about one hundred and eighty feet long, thirty wide in the broadest part, and in the loftiest, as we guessed, about thirty high. It was now dry, but at high tide the sea rises in it near six feet. Here is saw what I had never seen before, limpets and mussels in their natural state . . . We then walked through a natural arch in the rock, which might have pleased us by its novelty, had the stones which encumbered our feet, given us leisure to consider it. We were shown the gummy seed of the kelp, that fastens itself to a stone, from which it grows into a strong stalk.' It would seem that the Doctor was somewhat disgruntled despite the novelty of seeing limpets and kelp. Perhaps he was disappointed at not hearing the 'powerful reverberation of sounds', the famous echo of the pipes playing in fairyland which visitors to the cave are promised.

Skye has perhaps less to offer speleologists than other islands in the Hebrides, but amateurs of Jacobite history at any rate will want to see another of Strathaird's caves, about a mile south of Elgol, where Prince Charles Edward is said to have lain concealed in July 1746 before he was rowed back to the mainland. Still another group of caves, this time on the opposite coast near Portree, which in spite of the name given them did not shelter the Prince, is nevertheless well worth a visit, if only for the five mile journey by boat which gives impressive views of the Storr.

During his stay in Skye, Walter Scott remained within reach of Dunvegan, and another sightseeing excursion took him to the two beautiful flat-topped mountains, Healaval Beg and Healaval More, which are more usually known as MacLeod's Tables. The road to Orbost runs by the Tables, which are easily climbed by a footpath from Varkasaig. But they are perhaps best seen across Loch Dunvegan when, on a still day, they are perfectly reflected in the water.

Many legends are attached to MacLeod's Tables. Once, for instance, it is said that they were ordinary peaks, changed by a miraculous earthquake into their present form. A clan chief who objected to St. Columba's mission of Christianisation ordered that no-one on the island should give him bed or board. But the two mountains disobeyed the chief's injunction and, flattened in a sudden avalanche of stones, offered their high plateaux to the Saint as a resting-place. But the tale that was told Walter Scott concerns the visit an early MacLeod paid to the Scottish court. The Highland laird cut a poor figure among the mighty Lowland nobles, who mocked his obvious lack of funds. During a banquet, they kept on inviting him to admire the great table with its splendid appointments and especially the fine candelabra which illuminated the feast. Had he anything on Skye to compare with such riches? Nettled by their taunts, MacLeod invited the King to come and see for himself. In the course of time, the King came to Dunvegan and, at nightfall, MacLeod led him up to the Tables where a feast had been spread. Behind each guest stood a tall clansman holding aloft a flaming torch. 'Have you at your court', asked MacLeod, 'a bigger table than this or finer candlesticks?' The tale is a pleasing one, and Walter Scott made use of it in the 'Legend of Montrose'.

A final landmark is associated with Dunvegan — the three rocks known as MacLeod's Maidens, which stand out to sea facing Bracadale at the southernmost tip of the Duirinish Peninsula. The largest rock stands alone, flanked by the two smaller ones which are joined together just above sea-level. The rocks have an evil reputation. They are said, truly enough, to have caused many a shipwreck and they are reputed to be the embodiment of the three Norse fates who, like the Roman Parcae, spun and cut the thread of life. Others represent them as the last of the Valkyries who fled at the approach of Christianity. Mermaids have been seen sitting at their feet and they are sometimes associated with the sea-god, Oegir, the Neptune of the northern seas. But the most likely account of why the Maidens got their name is based on an historic incident. The story goes that the fourth Chief of the MacLeods, John, was stabbed to death as he stepped aboard his galley to join his wife and two daughters who were already seated. As he fell, the crew rushed to his aid and, in the confusion, the oarless boat came adrift. The three women were swept out to sea and eventually wrecked off Idragill Point, where the Maidens commemorate their death.

Many poets, apart from Walter Scott, have celebrated the legends of Skye. It is perhaps most closely associated with James Mac-Pherson (1736-1796), who claimed to have translated from Gaelic originals the works of the great Irish warrior and bard, Ossian, who is thought to have lived in the third century. The appearance of MacPherson's epic, Fingal, in 1762 caused great excitement among the men of letters of his day. It was followed the next year by a sequel, Temora, and both poems were much admired. But their authenticity was questioned, notably by Dr. Johnson. MacPherson was challenged to disclose his sources and eventually he produced what purported to be the original texts. They proved to have been forged or at least largely fabricated. But forger or not, MacPherson was a fine poet and his work lives on. Although Fingal's Cave is in Staffa, in the southern Hebrides, Skye, too, has its Fingal's Mount, a tall hill which makes a pleasant walk from Portree. But it is with another of MacPherson's heroes that the island is most closely associated. We have already met

Cuchullin at Dunscaith, where in the Ossianic cycle, he eventually marries the fair Bragela and leaves her to mourn him as he sails away to do battle against the Norse king. He never returns and looking out from that watch-tower, Bragela sings:

'Is it the white wave or the rock
And not Cuchillin's sails?
Often do the white mists deceive me for the
ship of my love.'

Like many another hero of his day, Cuchullin was a mighty hunter and, near Dunscaith, tourists are shown the great stone where he used to tie up his favourite dog, Luath, after the chase was over. From Ireland, Cuchullin, crossing the sea in two giant strides, set foot on Skye at Talisker Head, then fought 'for a day and a night and another day' on Broc-Bheinn in the Cuillins before gaining acceptance in the island. And it is in the Cuillins themselves that the legendary Irish hero is best remembered, for the name of the mountains is said to be no more than a corruption of 'Cuchullin'. In fact, some of the islanders still call the range the Cuchullins, using Coolins or Cuillins only as a convenient anglicism.

MacPherson's Fingal deals with the legends that once united Ireland and the Hebrides, while Walter Scott's 'Lord of the Isles' takes up Skye's history at the point where, in the 13th century, Somerled, Lord of Argyll, took control. Before then the Hebrides, which had been converted to Christianity in the 6th century by St. Columba, had been ruled by the Norse Kings as a powerful dominion which often endangered Scotland itself. In the 9th century, Kenneth MacAlpin had reigned over a small Scottish kingdom which united the Picts with the Scots. In the following centuries, the territories of Lothian and Strathclyde were annexed. Then in 1034 Duncan (the historic Duncan slain by Shakespeare's Macbeth) became the first King of Scotland. But after his death the throne was weakened by the rival claims to it of the Houses of Moray and Atholl. And it wasn't until the 13th century that a Scottish King was powerful enough to defeat — at Largs in 1263 — the combined forces of the Norwegians who were in alliance with the ruler of Skye and take possession of the Western Isles. Skye itself remained an appendage of the Earls of Ross, who intermarried with the MacDonalds and held the title of Lord of the Isles, until the 15th century when it reverted to the Scottish crown. The old title itself is still extant — one of many traditional courtesy titles held by the male heir to the British throne.

The ancient lore of the islands, which combines Celtic and Scandinavian mythology, was bound to appeal to Walter Scott who, as a child, had first heard of fairyland from the folk-tales collected by the Lowland poet, Thomas the Rhymer. He had lived in the 13th century and was believed to have been granted the gift of poetry by the fairies themselves. But his 'Lord of the Isles' is something of an exception, for in most of his best works he turned for inspiration to a later time when the customs, habits and traditions of the Highlands had fully matured and become part of Scotland's national heritage. That his heart was truly in the Highlands he proved to great effect when he master-minded the visit that his patron, friend and admirer, the Prince Regent, paid to Edinburgh in 1822, after his accession to the throne as King George IV. It was the first time for more than 200 years that a British King had come to Scotland and both the royal visitor and his master of ceremonies were determined to make the occasion a fully Scottish one. The King disembarked at Leith, Edinburgh's sea port, and caused great enthusiasm by displaying his vast bulk in full Scottish regalia. There was twenty stone to cram into the kilt but between them the King and his tailors managed it somehow. A letter written from Edinburgh on the 17th August and preserved in the Creevey Papers describes the occasion: 'He has been received by the people in the most respectful and orderly manner. All have turned out in their holiday clothes, and in numbers which are hardly credible'. The people cheered, the gentlemen attended the King's levee, the ladies were presented, the bands played. Walter Scott had written to all his large Highland acquaintance to summon them to the capital for the royal festivities. In the event the Highland presence was such that his son-in-law and famous biographer, John Gibson

70

Lockhart protested on behalf of his fellow Lowlanders that the monarch would be led to believe that Scotland started at the Grampians. And among the Highland contingent was The MacLeod of MacLeod, come from Skye with a hundred pipers.

The ancient art of playing the pipes was practised in Skye by the MacCrimmons of Boreraig who served the MacLeods as hereditary pipers since the earliest times. We do not know for certain where the family came from, but an old tradition believes that they held land in Harris before the Norsemen came to Skye. Magic is made to account for their musical genius which passed from father to son through the generations, and it is one more splendid fairytale to add to the island's large repository.

The first MacCrimmon piper — so the story goes — was an uninspired player, though he was competent enough to found a college of piping at Boreraig, where he taught many pupils, including his own son. The boy was assiduous, but he knew that he had not talent enough to achieve his ambition of succeeding his father as piper to the MacLeods. A competition to recruit the best young player was about to be held, and one day as the boy was practising hard on the hillside above the village, he lost heart and flung his pipes away. Then the hillside opened and a lovely lady appeared who offered him a silver chanter. He fitted it to his pipes and suddenly found himself playing the music that a local poet has called the 'sea-voice and hill-voice and moor-voice of Scotland'. A condition was attached to his owning the magic chanter; many years later when he had come to manhood and achieved his ambition to become head piper to his Chief, he was called upon to fulfil it. He heard the fairies' summons and, leaving his fireside and family, walked away and was never seen again. The tale is common enough in Scotland — it is told of Thomas the Rhymer whose genius was also on loan from fairyland. But the fact remains that from father to son the MacCrimmons remained pipers to the MacLeods until the '45. Then, it is said that the chief made MacCrimmon join a small force that he was sending in support of the Hanoverians. (It was then not uncommon for the lairds to play safe by backing both sides, nor for the septs of the same clan to join opposing factions). MacCrimmon had the Gaelic second sight and he foresaw his own death. He was killed in a skirmish, but first he composed the MacCrimmons' Lament, with its haunting refrain:

'No more, no more, nor more for ever
In war or peace shall MacCrimmon return'

With his death, the MacCrimmon Pipers and their college came to an end, too soon for Walter Scott to do more than lead the way for all the tourists who come to visit the old 'Pipers' Land' at Boreraig , where a monument stands to the MacCrimmons' memory. The centre of piping has now moved inland and bands of pipers come skirling across the bridge at Eilean Donan, the 13th century Jacobite stronghold which stands on its own island where the waters of the three lochs, Duich, Alsh and Long, meet.

But the road to Boreraig is still worth taking. It runs along the north coast of Glendale between steep hills and the shores of Loch Dunvegan, past Colbost and its offshore islands, past Tokaig, then down through a wooded valley and up again, winding steeply to the village, and past the Pipers' land to Boreraig's other curiosity, the so-called Manners Stone. This ancient boulder is thought to have played the principal part in a Celtic rite intended to correct those who had broken the social code, rather as England's ducking-stool was used to teach a lesson to nagging women.

Adjoining Boreraig is the tiny township of Galtrigill, the birthplace of Bonnie Prince Charlie's pilot, Donald MacLeod. After the Prince had made his escape, Donald was arrested on Benbecula and served a term of rigorous imprisonment on the hulks at Tilbury. He was released under the amnesty of 1747 and returned to die in his native village. To mark the ten weeks of his faithful service to the Prince, an admirer had presented him with a handsome silver snuff-box which was inscribed, 'Donald MacLeod of Gualtergill, in the Isle of Skye, the faithful Palinurus'. His fate was a sad one, for he had given up a profitable business to serve his Prince and he died in distress. Galtrigill, too, has come to a sad end: it was once a thriving community with its own peat moor, but a good modern road and piped water passed it by and it is now virtually uninhabited.

Skye is full of memories of the Jacobites of 1745 — of those who lived to tell the tale of those troubled times to their grandchildren and of those who fell fighting for the Stuarts' lost cause. For a man of Skye to die in battle was no unusual fate, since many Highlanders had long ago adopted the profession of arms and made their name as fine soldiers. As early as 1694, John Evelyn wrote in his Diary: 'Some regiments of Highland dragoons were on the march through England; they were of large stature, well appointed and disciplined.' He goes on to praise the boldness as well as the great strength of one of them: taking on two passing Dutchmen who had doubted his courage, he 'struck off the head of one, and cleft the head of the other down to the chin'. Such doughty fighters were never short of work, and the old Highland and Hebridean names are prominent on the roll-call of famous battlefields from Fontenoy to Brandywine. There was no shortage of wars and in an age of mercenaries, a man could choose his side — Ogilvy's Scots Regiment was based in France and Napoleon's Marshal MacDonald was born in the Long Island. No press-gang was needed in the Hebrides where an able-bodied young man would rather follow the fortunes of war than face starvation at home. Scotland had no Poor Law as such and charity was administered at random by the Church out of the pockets of the devout. One result of this haphazard policy was the army of 'sorners' — beggars turned highwaymen and worse — that terrified the countryside of solitary farms and lonely clachans, hamlets of no more than two or three dwellings, in the days of Queen Anne. 'Black' year followed black year, when the harvest lay sodden in the fields and the cattle died for lack of fodder. To make matters worse, there were many more mouths to feed. Throughout the 18th century, the population grew apace. It came near to doubling in England and Wales, rising from 5,500,000 in 1701 to over 9,000,000 a 100 years later. Much of this increase was due to a surge in medical science, ably assisted by such Scotsmen as Sir John Pringle, the Hunter brothers and William Smellie. There was besides far more concern for the sick — most of London's great hospitals were built, or, like St. Thomas', rebuilt before 1745. After 1780, the death rate, which had been declining in the last 50 years, fell by leaps and bounds once Jenner discovered the smallpox vaccine and put an end to a scourge which had taken a heavy toll of generation after generation in the manner of the great medieval plagues. The sad tale of emigration from the Highlands and Islands is largely one of failed harvests, but several turning-points mark its course. The first wave of evictions followed the Jacobite attempt in 1715 after which a number of estates were forfeited and became Crown property, administered from London. Sometimes the Commissioners encouraged the tenants and granted them longer leases than they had held from the old lairds, but this enlightened policy was relatively rare. All too often the estate was treated as a mere source of revenue and crofters who could not pay their way were turned off. In Skye, the MacDonald estates in Bracadale suffered badly and one township disappeared completely for a time when the people of Orbost went as a community to Australia. The situation took a turn for the worse after the '45 and the disappearance of the tacksmen. By abolishing the lairds' hereditary privileges, the new laws, passed after the final defeat of the Stuarts, destroyed the whole clan system of which the tacksmen in charge of the estates were an integral part. In the feudal world which survived until Culloden, a chief valued his men more than his land: his position and importance were judged by the number of his retainers even long after these had lost their value as fighting men in local feuds. As a result, anyone who claimed to be a gentleman kept up the largest retinue possible, both on his land and in his household. Servants were ill-paid: as Thomas Pennant tells it: 'The common servants have thirty shillings per annum, house, garden, six bolls of meal and shoes. The dairy maids thirteen shillings and fourpence and shoes: the common drudges, six and eightpence and shoes'. The Lewis farmer who paid these rates in 1772 kept a staff of 17, and we hear of bonnet lairds, worth £50 a year or less, with a household of 20. This extravagant love of feudal show may have been obsolete, but it had one advantage —

it kept people at work. And once the old landlordism disappeared, the tacksmen and their chiefs became mere 'traffickers in land', as Dr. Johnson called them. He resumed the problem succinctly: 'The Chiefs, divested of their privileges, necessarily turned their thought to the improvement of their lands, and expect more rent as they have less homage'. As rents rose in the second half of the 18th century, the standard of life at the top followed suit; at the bottom, the miserable livelihood of the poor people declined still further. Figures for emigration speak for themselves: in the 20 years from 1763, contemporaries estimated that 30,000 people sailed to America from the Hebrides. The American Wars of Independence slowed down the momentum, but the figures rose again in the '80s. The next upsurge in emigration came at the end of the Napoleonic Wars, a period of peace which was not one of plenty for the officers on half-pay and the demobilised men. It coincided with several seasons of bad harvests and a severe trade depression. From some 2,000 people leaving in 1802, official statistics show nearly 30,000 emigrated in one single year in 1818 and about 35,000 in 1819, chiefly to Canada, which was then British territory. But the true number of emigrants may well be nearly double, for many left from small ports where no tally was taken and Scotland's long coastline encouraged cargo ships to pick up emigrants out of sight of the excise men.

A final change to the domestic economy of the Islands came with the clearances which led to the removal of whole communities of crofters and a further wave of emigration. In 1841, the population of Skye was over 23,000; a 100 years later, after the Second World War, it had dropped to 8,000. The principle of sheep farming was in itself excellent, for the island's grazing was well suited to it — the trouble was that it fell entirely into the hands of sheep-farmers from the south who moved in with their shepherds and their flocks on to land relinquished to them in exchange for the high rents they were prepared to pay. Even the townships lost their communal grazing lands. The islanders fought back and 'land reform' meetings were held on Fairy Bridge. The resistance, strongest in Glendale and Trotternish, culminated in the 'Battle of the Braes' where the crofters armed with sticks and stones turned back police sent from Glasgow to evict them. There were broken heads and bloody noses and, though no life was lost, a Royal Commission was set up which resulted in the Crofters' Act of 1886. They call it the Crofters Magna Carta because for the first time in their history, the crofters were given their rights, including security of tenure. The last battle to be fought on Scottish soil was a victory.

Car Excursions

Speleologists can spend a pleasant day on Strathaird down in the south-west visiting Skye's most interesting caves.

Elgol: is the best centre to see the most famous, the **Spar Cave.** Elgol is a 30 mile return journey from Broadford, along the 881, through Kilbride and Torrin. From there a minor road leads to Glanaskille, north of Strathaird Point. From the village a motor boat can usually be hired to explore the Spar and the tour prolonged perhaps to take in Prince Charlie's Cave on the other side of the point.

Harlosh's small peninsula reaches out into Loch Bracadale between two little lochs, Caroy and Vatten, off the 863 which joins Dunvegan to Sligachan. This district which is associated with the Dunvegan pipers is rather inaccessible to cars because the roads that cover it are little more than winding tracks and turnings are easy to miss. So the best way to explore the caves is again by motor boat, crossing to the Duirinish coast to include the fine Archway caves at Greep, on the point to the south of Orbost. Here in the neighbourhood of Duirinish and Dunvegan are two well-known sites: **MacLeods Tables,** easily climbed on foot, are reached from Varkasaig which is on a secondary road leading south from Orbost through the glen. **MacLeods Maidens** stand offshore at Idrigill Point, the southernmost of the Duirinish peninsula, some five miles due south of Greep, but there is no road suitable for cars. A final drive from Dunvegan through glorious scenery takes one along the coastal road B884 which runs up the north coast of Duirinish to Boreraig and on to Galtrigill, just south of Dunvegan Head.

Cuillins from Elgol

Ridge Cuillins

Blaven and Loch Slapin

The Quiraing

To reach **Glenbrittle,** Skye's climbing centre (about 12 miles from Sligachan), take the 863 to Drynoch, and before reaching the town, bear left (south) at the junction for Carbost and left again following the signpost to Glenbrittle. The road runs through the Glen within full view of the Cuillins. From Glenbrittle it is sometimes possible to take motorboat trips to the outlying Isle of Soay, as well as to Rum, Eigg and Canna.

BLACKHOUSE MUSEUM
SKYE

Pleasure Island

'Primroses and bluebells are followed by honeysuckle and roses; then comes the mass of blossoms of a west coast July . . . hardhead and scabious, orchis and pansy, meadowsweet and asphodel, carpets of eyebright and milkwort and thyme, and later heather, nuts and rowanberries'. The road, or rather the track, that leads down from Orbost to the sandy beach at Varkasaig is lovely at all seasons, says Otta Swire, who has collected the legends of Skye. But she is dealing in hard fact when she describes the rich tapestry of wild flowers which are spread out for our delight from April to October.

Although Skye is well on the way to Greenland, its climate is not as rigorous as its proximity to the Arctic circle might suggest for the Hebrides have the good fortune to lie in the path of the Gulf Stream whose North Atlantic Drift does much to temper the weather. The temperature seldom drops below freezing point; what frosts there are last a few days only and though snow caps the Cuillins it never lies on the ground heavily or for long. As Dr. Johnson wrote: 'The winter of the Hebrides consists of little more than rain and wind. As they are surrounded by an ocean never frozen, the blasts that come over to them across the water are too much softened to have the power of congelation. The salt loughs or inlets of the sea, which shoot very far into the island, never have any ice on them and the pools of fresh water will never bear the walker. The snow that sometimes falls is soon dissolved by the air, or the rain'. In Skye there is nothing of the rugged Highland winter which lasts so late into the spring; the Inner Islands are milder than anywhere else in Britain and they compare favourably with the south-west of England, Wales and Ireland.

With a rainfall of 120 inches, the Western Highlands are reputed to be the wettest region in Europe, but the heavy rainbelt misses the coast and comes in to break on the high mountains of the hinterland. In Skye, the average rainfall is no more than 40 to 60 inches, rising to 80 inches on the highest ground. In summer, the sun shines hot: the long-term average for the month of May is 200 hours, with a wealth of spring flowers to prove it. In winter, it is such islands as Barra, Lewis and the bird sanctuary of St. Kilda which get the full force of the gales, when violent gusts have been known to lift the sea-wrack over cliffs 600 ft high. The credulous believe the worst of these storms are sent with a special purpose . . . to carry away the soul of a dying monarch. But although Skye itself is protected from extremes by the outlying barrier of the Long Island, thick shoes and rainproof clothing are needed as protection against the island's two enemies: mist dissolving into sudden showers and almost constant wind. The wind blows continuously even in the inner islands and makes sun-bathing precarious on the fine sands that line the coasts. It also affects evaporation, determining the character of the local flora, and has much to do with the mists.

Misty Isle is one of Skye's many nicknames, and climbers are always being warned against the perils of sudden fogs descending and blocking their way. But, then, it is the mist that shapes and reshapes the landscape, filters the light that plays on hill and heath, gives depth and colour to the waters of sea and loch. And when it lifts and the rain stops, there appear those spectacular Hebridean rainbows that make the end of a shower doubly welcome. Rainbows, and in the autumn when the moorland turns red and gold, there is an occasional chance to see the Aurora Borealis and the fireworks of the Northern Lights, that the islanders call by their old Norse name the 'Merry Dancers'.

The season in Skye starts in the spring, and that is the time of year that many tourists prefer, when the islands regain a new freshness as the dark winter time recedes and the days grow longer and longer until, in the high summer, it is possible to read without a light long into the night. The smoothest crossings are also made in the spring, though even then freak weather may give bad sailors an uneasy trip. From May till October, the Caledonian-MacBrayne service is fullest, but in the summer holiday months, the ferries become crowded. Then, from the middle of September, crossings are fewer and the daily itinerary no longer includes the more remote islands (see page 16).

For climbers on Skye there is no particular season. They come for the Cuillins — the great horseshoe ridge of black peaks with their neighbour, the massive Red Hills. The highest tops nearly all reach to over 3,000 ft and the whole range fills the narrow neck of Skye between Lochs Scavaig and Brittle on the west coast and runs eastward up to Sligachan and Broadford. The official guide book tells us that the Cuillin Hills are 'unquestionably the most difficult and savage range in the British Isles'. They are certainly among the most beautiful. The tourist arriving in Skye is confronted at once with the island's most spectacular landmark, and without any intention of adventuring towards the summits, soon learns to distinguish the dark peaks of the Main Ridge and recognise the sunset glow that the Red Cuillins throw off. Much of their beauty they owe to their geological formation — the Cuillins originated in a vast upswelling of volcanic lava which covered Skye in the Tertiary Age. It is black basalt which crowns the high peaks of the main range, notably on Sgurr Alasdair, at 3,251 ft the highest peak on Skye, and its slightly smaller neighbour, Sgurr Tearlach. Later formations of crystalline rock — granite in the Red Hills, gabbro in the main mass — give the hills the lovely variety of their colouring, as well as a special character that experienced climbers will appreciate. Turning to the guidebook again, we read that gabbro, of which the Cuillins have the largest area in the British Isles, is 'the perfect mineral answer to the rock climber's prayer'. It is a hard, unyielding rock which, in these highlands, is split by layers of the softer

80

basalt which, in turn, forms the greater part of the gentler slopes. Finally, the action of frost and ice through the ages account for the rough scree which covers the mountainside, with its heavy (and dangerous) scattering of loose stones. And it is frost and ice again which have shaped the circular corries and splintered the peaks above the rockface which glaciers had once worn smooth and round.

Somewhat to the south of the Main Ridge, between the heads of Loch Slapin and Loch Scavaig, rises an outpost of the Black Cuillins, Blaven. The highest summits of this group — made up by Garbh-bhenn, Sgurr nam Each, Clach Glos and Blaven itself — are 3,000 ft above sea level and offer magnificent views of the serried ranks of peaks in the main group, with the seascape and the smaller islands out to the south as a backdrop.

To give advice to mountaineers is quite beyond the compass of this guidebook — and the knowledge of its author. But the hill ranges of Skye are accessible to a stout walker and even some of the most spectacular summits are within his reach — if, that is, he is able to keep up a steady pace for four or six hours walking. The best bases from which to approach the western Cuillins are Glenbrittle, where there is a Youth Hostel which includes a climbing school, or the charming hotel at Sligachan.

A first and fairly easy climb leads to the top of Bruach na Frithe, which rises to over 3,000 ft. A clear track starts by the cairns at the end of the glen road, then leads gently upwards towards the summit with its panorama of mountains, glens and sea. A number of Cuillin peaks require hard scrambling and are not listed, since this is specialist work, but the highest of them all, Sgurr Alasdair, can be reached by the well-worn track to the Lagan corrie. For those ambitious to reach the very top, there remains a tough walk by the little lake and the Great Stone Shoot, then a final short but steep scramble to the very top.

Another famous peak, Sgurr Dearg can be tackled from the approach to Coire Lagan, over the broad shoulder of Sron Dearg.

But the route is complicated and the first attempt is best made with a guide. One reward that the mountain offers is a close-up view of the Inaccessible Peak, rising sheer and still unscaled. All visitors to Skye will sooner or later hear of Sgurr nan Gillean, but although its ascent presents no especial dangers, the shortest route to the top is hard to find and first efforts to chart it generally end up in much uncomfortable scrambling through very tough scree to recover the straight line. Again, not recommended without a practised guide.

The Blaven, too, is beyond the powers of all but experienced climbers, who know the mountain. Its southern slope, however, is an exception: it provides what is little more than a pleasant long walk from Camasunary. The Blaven itself is somewhat out of the way, but buses run near it from Broadford to Loch Slapin.

To hardy walkers as opposed to climbers deserving the name of mountaineers, it is the high hills of Trotternish in the -north of Skye which have most to offer, with the Quiraing corrie in the north and the Storr 12 miles to the south. Here are many famous beauty spots — the Kilt Rock formed of black dolerite in vertical bands which suggest the pleats of a kilt just sweeping the turbulent sea below, and, most famous of all, the Old Man of Storr, a basalt monolith 160 ft high, in shape like a giant avocado pear balancing precariously on its rocky plinth. Travelling by road north from Portree, it first appears over the Brothers' Bay, surmounting a mass of weird rock-towers, pillars, pinnacles and cliffs to which local fancy has given appropriate names: the Old Man's wife, his dog, his castle and its many retainers. The Old Man himself seems to achieve a miracle of balance and, since the rock overhangs its own base, it is practically inaccessible, but a rough scramble up the hillside brings one to its base. No further, for it must again be stressed that rock climbing in the Storr, as well as in the Quiraing, is *out*. The whole region is composed of volcanic basalt, a notoriously unreliable rock where even hill walkers kicking a few loose stones may still provoke a landslide.

Perhaps the best approach to the Storr, however, is from the west, from Loch Snizort (Youth Hostel) along Glen Haltin and its river, then up Lon Mor and along the so-called 'Backbone of Trotternish'. To the east of the ridge, the volcanic range drops 600 ft to a corrie which is one of the most freakishly splendid sights that the Scottish mountains have to offer. Guarded by a weird assembly of basalt pinnacles — one of them is a corkscrew 100 ft high pierced as it were by windows — it is floored with the brightest of green grass where the botanist comes into his own among the wealth of wild flowers. There are the purple saxifrage, Alpine Lady's Mantle, the uncommon hairy rock cress, pink saw-wort, the sedum known as rose-root and the buttercup called globe flower. There grows — uniquely in the British Isles, so it is thought — the Icelandic purslane with its tiny white trefoil flowers.

There are splendid walks too in the Quiraing. This small northern range, which overlooks the Flodigarry landslip, is enclosed between the cliff rocks of Meall na Suireamaich and a wall of lava towers which separate it from the coast. At its centre stands the Table, a crag with a flat top 100 yards long and 40 yards wide, guarded by an obelisk called the Needle, itself 100 ft tall. A track from the highest point of the Uig-Staffin road leads to it through a space between the rockface and the lower reef, not unsuitably styled The Prison.

This strange landscape has about it something unreal. It does not belong to the workaday world, and it is an amusing coincidence to find it described by Alice in Wonderland herself. In 1878, the little girl, for whom Lewis Carroll also invented magic adventures Beyond the Looking-Glass, had grown into a rather prosaic young lady. Alice Liddell was 26 when she visited Skye with her family. In her diary ('diary writing was very much the thing to do'), she describes an outing to the Quiraing. The ladies went in their carriage, accompanied on foot by one Rory MacLeod as guide. However, they were not spared 'the difficult climb' up into the 'wonderful rock'. 'The view between the sheer sides to the valley below was beautiful', writes Miss Liddell. She had not the words to describe it; indeed, it is indescribable.

Spring is the time to botanise in the Quiraing and the Cuillins, where the purple saxifrage is out as early as March. The white Star saxifrage follows in May and June and, in a thick cushion of rose-red florets, the Moss Campion. Then, a rare plant is sometimes found near the lochs, Eriocaulon, or Pipewort, which closely resembles the lovely blue-flowered Water Lobelia, which is itself quite common near mountain lakes. In the limestone of the south, Mountain Avens grow here at sea level, followed as spring turns to summer by Guelder Roses and the Helleborines of the orchis family.

From May onwards, long coastal stretches of the machair are taken over by wild flowers — in such profusion that the term grass normally given to this rough pasture-land no longer seems apposite. Protected from the sea by a belt of marram grass, whose tough creeping roots fix the sand, the turf of the machair is rich in trefoils and clovers, and their powerful scent is carried far on the wind. Then, in seasonal order, come buttercups and daisies, blue Speedwell, yellow Birdsfoot and golden Dandelion, the Eyebright with its lavender flowers, harebells and wild thyme, pansies yellow and violet and the bright potentilla, called Silverweed. The summer machair on Skye is a rare enough sight to tempt one to travel out further to enjoy it where it is at its best — in the unbroken solitude of the Outer Hebrides. As summer advances, Scotland's heathers bloom — the common ling, the cross-leaved variety in marshy grounds and, on the sunny slopes, the purple grapes of bell heather.

The Hebrides as a whole constitute a natural bird sanctuary, with St. Kilda's, far out in the Atlantic, providing the world's greatest gannetry. But seabirds need solitude and in Skye nowadays they pass through rather than settle. Yet there are breeding grounds not far off. In spring, in the nesting season, puffins burrow out their nests in the turf on top of the cliffs. There are colonies of these comic descendents of the Great Auk, now sadly extinct, in the outlying islands, in the Ascribs and Fladda-Chuain off the north of Trotternish. Belonging to the same family, the brown guillemot and the black razorbill breed more widely and are often seen flying over Skye. Other seabirds uncommon to the mainlander are the petrels, which include the Manx Shearwater, which has its breeding grounds on Rum, Eigg and Canna, the Storm Petrel and the spectacular Fulmar. This large round-headed bird, not unlike a vast gull, has in the last 100 years extended its breeding grounds from St. Kilda and become fairly common all round the British coast. In Skye, it has established several colonies, where in common with other petrels it lays its single egg. The green cormorant and the Shags have also settled in Skye; herring-gulls frequent Portree harbour and, as is the custom of gulls, follow the steamer to and fro from Mallaig.

All year round, Skye has its full complement of land and fresh-water birds: oystercatchers and sandpipers, redshanks and dippers on the beaches and on the lochs, flotillas of duck, shelduck and mallard as well as teal and coot, and crossing the smooth waters, a slow progress of swans. On freshwater lochs early visitors to Skye, arriving before April may catch a glimpse of the Whooper Swan which nests in Iceland but, along with the Snow Buntings, winters in Skye. But one must wait for the autumn, late September and October for the magnificent sight of migrating geese when, at sundown, great gaggles of Whitefronts, Barnacles and Greylogs fly in formation across the sky.

The glory of Skye's bird flock remains the Golden Eagle. Now strenuously protected, the greatest of eagles is still threatened — as was the beautiful white-tailed Sea Eagle whose last nest on Skye was recorded in Glen Sligachan more than 50 years ago. Yet the Golden Eagle can be seen planing over the scree, or solitary on a rocky perch high up in the Cuillins, outlined against the sky. Now it is in danger from the modern chemical pesticides which are also damaging the chances of breeding ospreys again.

Man has always been nature's fiercest enemy, but is at last and late in the day doing his best to repair the harm he has done. Bird and beast are protected — already on the sunny moorland slopes the red grouse has come to join Scotland's speckled ptarmigan which has its natural habitat on the stony scree, and the red deer is back in some numbers, now that the Forestry Commission is working to restore the island's plundered forests.

When in the 18th century travellers to the Highlands deplored the lack of timber, what they missed were the fine plantations of deciduous hardwoods which graced the great English estates, for Skye — which had once formed part of the Great Caledonian Forest — in those days still had plenty of woodland. Even within living memory, cattle were sent out to pasture with cowbells round their necks lest they should wander out of sight into the trees. There are in fact few of the common trees — aspen, alder, yew, willow, oak and ash — which do not grow freely in Scotland. They have been joined through the ages by such foreign imports as birch from England, plane and sycamore from France, larch from the Tyrol, spruce from Norway and a number of colonial woods, all of which have acclimatised themselves readily enough. But centuries of thoughtless tree-felling have left their scars: the earliest settlers, Gaels, Angles and Norsemen, cut down the trees and burned them for the wood-ash they used as manure; the flocks and herds which were taken high up into the summer hills overcropped the moor and damaged seedlings and, even where whole forests were enclosed for the pleasure of the Royal hunts, the red deer and roebuck did much harm by stripping bark from the saplings. Then industry came to finish off what poor farming methods had started: the early shipyards on the Clyde devoured whole forests of native oak as well as pine, floated down from the Highlands, and tree bark was in great demand for the tanning of leather, and iron-smelting depended on tree charcoal. Because of these depredations, the modern tourist on Skye is confronted by acres of barren glen and moor where once grew forests of birch and hazel. The Forestry Commission — set up by an Act of Parliament in 1919 — has taken over some 10,000 acres on Skye and now has a fine plantation on the hillside at Glenbrittle, but its choice of trees is limited by the demands of industry for softwood. So firs and more firs are planted to supply the needs of the sawmill and paper manufactory at Fort William. New varieties are introduced — the Lodgepole

Pine and the Satka Spruce as well as the Japanese Larch — but the general effect remains monotonous, and the tourist who wants to get an idea of what the woods of Skye were once like must walk under the ancestral trees of Dunvegan and Armadale.

Although modern forestry has its aesthetic limitations, it does provide the islanders with much-needed employment and, along with tourism, makes it possible for them to pursue to some extent their traditional way of life. Many measures have been taken this century to make crofting viable, chiefly by dividing state-owned land into economically rational units, but the nature of the soil, the climate, the isolation of the Hebrides with the transport costs their relative inaccessibility entails, all combine to prevent island farming from ever becoming a full-time occupation. Even modern crofters must have a secondary source of income.

As we know, fishing was tried, but failed. In the fairly recent past, Lord Leverhulme of Port Sunlight fame, spent huge sums in attempting to transform Stornoway on Lewis into a great northern fishing centre, but his plans went awry and the project had to be abandoned. Then came the long years of the Depression, and after the Second World War, economic and political moves combined to defeat the Hebridean trawlers. Now modern methods of deep sea fishing on an international scale as well as the continuing search for North Sea oil stand in the way of local enterprise. On the other hand, there has been a recent revival of inshore fishing, which is also available as a tourist sport, with good fun to be had for those hardy enough to embark on the prawn fishing expeditions round Uig. For the more sedentary, there is good fishing in rivers and freshwater lochs, notably on the Hinnisdal river, on the Skeabost and the Sligachan, among many others, as well as in the Staffin lochs and in the Sleat district. The main hotels handle fishing rights — salmon as well as trout — and with the Tourist Offices, make arrangements for would-be anglers.

Then, there are boats for hire in Portree Bay and, in the south, from Isle Ornsay off Sleat. But the coast of Skye is extremely dangerous, with rocks as well as tidal rapids and it must again be stressed that only experienced navigators should set out unaccompanied. Weather permitting, there is good bathing too in the sandy bays of Tarskavaig, Torrin and Staffin, from the beach at Harlosh and, of course, from the famous Coral Beach. Active tourists will find tennis courts at Portree and, since we are in Scotland, golf courses (mainly 9 holes) within reach of the capital, and of Broadford and Sconser. The Skye Highland Games are held in summer (generally in August), with piping and dancing, and ceilidhs are put on during the season. But these entertainments are remote indeed from the original fireside gatherings where neighbours got together to gossip and sing the old songs, as the moonshine whisky circulated late into the night.

A far more genuine entertainment is to be found in shopping for the island's main product — its handmade woollens and knitwear. The story of Harris tweed itself belongs to the Long Island. It goes back nearly a century, for it was in the 1880s that the Countess of Dunmore first encouraged its manufacture by marketing it in London. The fame of Harris tweed is now world-wide and its export makes an important contribution to the national economy. A stop has been put to the many attempts made to infringe the patent by a court ruling in 1964, which gave an official description of the genuine product. 'A tweed made from pure virgin wool, produced in Scotland, spun, dyed and finished in the Outer Hebrides, and hand-woven by the islanders at their own homes in the islands of Lewis, Harris, Uist, Barra and their several appurtenancies, and all known as the Outer Hebrides'.

But Skye, too, has its tweeds (mills and showroom at Portree — open to visitors) made on the same principle, as well as a thriving knitwear industry. The work is carried out by the croftsmen's wives and their womenfolk, who knit at home the immense variety of the Islands' designs, which range from the prettily-coloured Fair Isles to the intricate patterns of Arran, where each cable twist recalls an incident in a family's history.

A full day on Skye is a reward in itself. And as the sun sinks in its splendour or twilight lingers on far into the night, there remains one pleasure to be enjoyed — a simple evening meal of traditional quality. To quote Dr. Johnson for the last time, 'He that shall complain of his fare in the Hebrides, has improved his delicacy more than his manhood'.

MᶜLEOD'S TABLES

Fine Island Fare

Not quite for the last time . . . for Dr. Johnson was gourmet enough to celebrate the best the Scottish table had to offer. 'If an epicure,' he wrote, 'could remove by a wish, in quest of sensual gratification, wherever he had supped he would breakfast in Scotland.'

Breakfasting in the Highlands is still a rare pleasure. I will not here engage in the controversy which rages over porridge—whether it should be eaten sitting or standing, hot or cold, taken with salt or with the added—some say effeminate—luxury of sugar and cream, but move straight on to its main course, the choice of which should form the first serious business of the day. To begin with, there is a variety of fish to choose from—Aberdeen haddock, better known as Finnan (from the village of Findon, so pronounced, in the Mearns where it was initially cured); fine kippers and sometimes the delicate copper-coloured Arbroath smokies. A piece of haddock, gently broiled in milk, then kept hot while an egg to top it is poached in the remaining liquid, sets a stout walker up for the day's excursion, but the old fish-wife's method of accommodating it as Finnan-haddie*** makes a good supper dish for a cold evening.

The best bacon in Scotland comes from Ayrshire and when it is on the menu provides a good excuse to indulge in fresh eggs, for in the Islands the hens still feed freely in the farmyard. To get its full flavour, as with all good bacon and ham, it should be grilled, not fried.

90

An unusual dish to make its appearance at the breakfast table is black pudding and, better still for amateurs, the herb-stuffed white pudding of the Shetlands, a speciality readily available at good grocers which, incidentally, travels reasonably well.

Substantial though a good Scottish breakfast is, it no longer includes the venison patties, the game pies, the smoked sides of salmon which were once common fare. And the large slices of cheese whose odour spoilt the fragrance of the tea for Dr. Johnson are no longer served in Scotland. But in other respects, the profusion of side-dishes remains the same—not merely bread or toast, but warm home-made scones, fresh baps***, slim oatmeal cakes, with butter, preserves, Scottish honey and marmalade arrive with the tea and coffee. The Hebrides have been acquainted with both for a very long time—while the 18th century Englishman was still drinking claret for his breakfast, tea and coffee came in duty free from Holland where there were no customs guards to exact the high imposts which made the price of both commodities prohibitive elsewhere.

Tea-time in the Highlands is no longer the Gargantuan meal it was before the Second World War, but on a wet afternoon it is still possible to steam off by an open coal fire while partaking of scones and jam and such delicacies as Dundee cake and petticoat tails***.

After a full Scottish breakfast, the best lunch in Scotland, as elsewhere in the British Isles, is often provided by the local pub, where, in lieu of sandwiches, oven-fresh baps serve to enfold ham off the bone or cheese. In a country short of pasture land, dairy herds are few and the variety of cheese consequently limited. Hotel cheese-boards are topped up by English and continental imports, and Stilton is served more commonly than the excellent Blue Highland. But the national cheese, the Dunlop, which is not unlike Cheddar, has a fine tang to it and a number of rich cream cheeses, which sometimes appear rolled in oats, are not to be despised for a midday snack. Some of the larger inns excel in simple hot dishes, a shepherd's or cottage pie, for instance, a hotch-potch*** or the Scotsman's alternative to the American hamburger or the Englishman's 'bangers and mash'—collops***, while hotel bars offer cold roast meats, with the added touch of home-made mayonnaise and vinaigrette to dress the salad stuffs.

Authorities on Scottish cooking insist that the old French tradition survives in the country's gastronomy, and it is certainly true that a large number of culinary terms as well as words in common use in house-keeping—itself called "menage" in Scotland as in France—are closer to the French language than to English. But it is perhaps in the care given to the preparation of the simplest ingredients that Scottish cooks come nearest to their continental counterparts. There is no question here of the so-called "haute cuisine": there is skill and to spare in accommodating fresh local produce rather than silver to lavish on importing foreign ingredients. Refrigeration has made its way to the Hebrides, but trout*** still comes fresh from the burn and fowl*** from the farmyard rather than pre-packed from the deep freeze, and excellent soups are home-made, using old-fashioned cuts of beef or mutton flavoured with fresh vegetables. The simple fare which can be enjoyed in the Highlands and Islands is becoming hard to find.

Recieces

Recipes

***

Baps: For 1lb flour, use 2oz of lard, 1oz of yeast and ¼pt of milk. Sift the flour into a warm bowl with a pinch of salt and rub in the lard. In another bowl, cream the yeast with a teaspoonful of sugar and half a pint of warm milk and water and strain into the flour, kneading the whole into a soft dough. Cover, and set to rise in a warm place for about an hour. Knead again lightly and divide into oval shaped pieces, about three inches long and two wide. Brush with a little milk and water and dust with flour. Place on a greased and floured oven tray and set to prove again for twenty minutes. Dust again with flour before baking for fifteen to twenty minutes in a hot oven.

Chicken Fillets with Egg Sauce: This dish can be made on its own, by poaching the fillets in a well-flavoured chicken broth, or more economically, by removing them from the bird used for a Cock-a-leekie soup (see below). In either case, some of the broth (or stock) should be kept to make the sauce. Egg-sauce: This is in fact a white sauce, made with half milk and half chicken stock, into which two hard-boiled eggs are chopped and a little parsley added before serving. Keep it thick enough to coat the chicken fillets and add some thick cream at the last moment.

Cock-a-Leekie: Best made in large quantities, with a boiling fowl, but you can get good results by using pieces of cut chicken, in the proportion of two pounds of meat to three or four of leeks. The fowl is poached gently and steadily in stock (or water if a whole fowl is used), flavoured with peppercorns, a clove and some mace as well as some sprigs of parsley. Add the coarse green part of the leeks, reserving the white which should be split 'en julienne' into inch lengths. Remove the meat when it is ready (about two hours), sieve the resulting broth into another pan, then add the julienne of leeks and cook on (for about an hour) until they are tender. Before serving add some of the chicken meat, cubed or minced. The soup should be thick with leeks. Some old recipes suggest the addition of a few dried prunes—after being soaked, they should be cooked in the broth for at least one hour.

Collops: One pound of steak minced, two onions and some mushrooms or mushroom ketchup. Fry the vegetables roughly chopped in a spoonful of smoking hot dripping, using a heavy stewpan. When brown, add the meat, with a little water, or gravy if you have it, flavour and leave to simmer for up to an hour, stirring from time to time to prevent the meat from forming lumps. Before serving, add half a cupful of fine breadcrumbs or a little oatmeal to absorb the liquid. Serve with slices of hard-boiled egg and triangles of fried bread, or more substantially, with a border of mashed potatoes.

Finnan Haddie: Cut the fish into convenient pieces and lay them in a deep frying pan with a large spoonful of butter, also cut up. Cover and steam gently for five minutes. Thicken a cupful of milk with some potato flour (in preference to cornflour) and pour the mixture over the fish. Stir carefully, allow to thicken and serve.

Hotch-Potch: This spring dish — half soup, half stew — depends for its excellence on the freshness of garden vegetables. It is usually made with two pounds of a cheap cut of mutton—neck, or perhaps shoulder. It is found in France, with an oxtail replacing the mutton, under the name of 'hochepot'. The vegetables, of which there should be double the weight of meat, can combine any or all of the following: carrots, turnips, peas, broad beans, cauliflower and/or white cabbage, *spring* onions. Put the meat, suitably cut up, into a heavy pan and cover with about four pints of cold water. Add salt, bring to the boil and skim. Then add the carrots and turnips, diced, and simmer for two hours, or more. The longer the soup is cooked, the better the flavour, but it should not be allowed to boil hard. An hour or so before serving, add the shelled peas, the shucked beans, florets of cauli- flower (previously cooked in cold salt water), the shredded cab- bage and, optionally, a little shredded lettuce. Cook on until the remaining vegetables are well done, then add the spring onions finely chopped. Before serving—with the meat in the middle of the tureen and the vegetables surrounding it—add some fresh chopped parsley. Classical cookery books tell us that the hotch- potch should be nearly as thick as porridge.

Petticoat Tails: There are innumerable recipes for various types of shortbread—this one is quickly made. To a pound and a half of flour take eight ounces of butter and three of fine caster sugar. Melt both in less than a quarter of a pint of milk, warmed but *not* boiled. Make a well in the centre of the flour, pour in, mix quickly and knead lightly. Leave for a while before rolling out—into a large thin circle. From the centre, using a deckle- edged flan ring (or if need be a large saucer), cut out a cake; then divide the outer circle into approximately eight fantails.

Cook in a moderate oven for up to thirty minutes, on paper laid on an oven tin. Serve with the round cake in the middle and the 'tails' as radii.

Scotch Broth: An economical soup since it requires relatively little meat, and a convenient one which improves with reheating. A pound of neck of mutton forms the basis. When the meat has been brought to the boil (in cold water) and skimmed, add two ounces each of split peas and barley which have been soaked overnight and leave to simmer for a couple of hours till both are tender. Then add a 'jardiniere' consisting of diced carrots and turnips, leek and onion and green cabbage (the latter shredded). Before serving, take out the meat, remove the bones and cut into neat pieces before returning to the soup. Serve very hot.

Trout: A simple Scottish way of dealing with trout fresh from the burn. Dip in seasoned milk, iced from the 'fridge; then roll in oats. Fry for a few minutes each side in a cast-iron pan (or one with a coated surface). Lard is the best medium to use as the fat must be very hot and butter blackens quickly.

A Short List of Island Hotels and Tourist Offices

ARDVASAR HOTEL	Ardvasar	Telephone	223
BROADFORD HOTEL	Broadford		204/5
DUNOLLIE HOTEL			253
DUNTULM CASTLE HOTEL	Duntulm		213/16
DUNVEGAN HOTEL	Dunvegan		202
MISTY ISLE HOTEL			208
WHITE HEATHER HOTEL	Kyleakin		277/287
ROYAL HOTEL	Portree		225/6
ROSEDALE			31
COOLIN HILLS HOTEL			- 3
SCONSER LODGE	Sconser	(Sligachan)	206
SKEABOST BRIDGE HOTEL	Skeabost		202
SLIGACHAN HOTEL	Sligachan		204
UIG HOTEL	Uig		205

YOUTH HOSTELS at Glenbrittle, Broadford, Raasay and Uig

TOURIST OFFICES: Isle of Skye Tourist Organisation, Meall House, PORTREE. Tel. 137

and information from: Skye Ferry Filling Station, Armadale Atholl Filling Station, Dunvegan

Tourist Office, BROADFORD Tel.361 (open May to October).

A Short List of Books

The Journal of a Tour to the Hebrides   James Boswell
(Pub. Dent)
Charles Edward Stuart   David Daiches
(Pub. Pan)
Tour through the Whole Island of Great Britain   Daniel Defoe
(Pub. Dent)
A Journey to the Western Islands of Scotland   Samuel Johnson
(Pub. O.U.P.)
Prince in the Heather   Eric Linklater
(Pub. Panther)
Life of Sir Walter Scott   J.G. Lockhart
(Pub. Dent)
The Enchanted Isles   A. Alpin MacGregor
(Pub. Joseph)
In Search of Scotland   H.V. Morton
(Pub. Methuen)
The Hebrides   W.H. Murray
(Pub. Heinemann)
Culloden   John Prebble
(Pub. Penguin)
The Highland Clearances   John Prebble
(Pub. Penguin)
Portrait of Skye and the Outer Hebrides   W.Douglas Simpson
(Pub. Hale)
Skye, the Island and its Legends   O.F. Swire
(Pub. Blackie)
Beyond the Highland Line   ed. A.J.Youngson
(three journals of travel in 18thC. Scotland)
(Pub. Collins)

Index

(People and places)

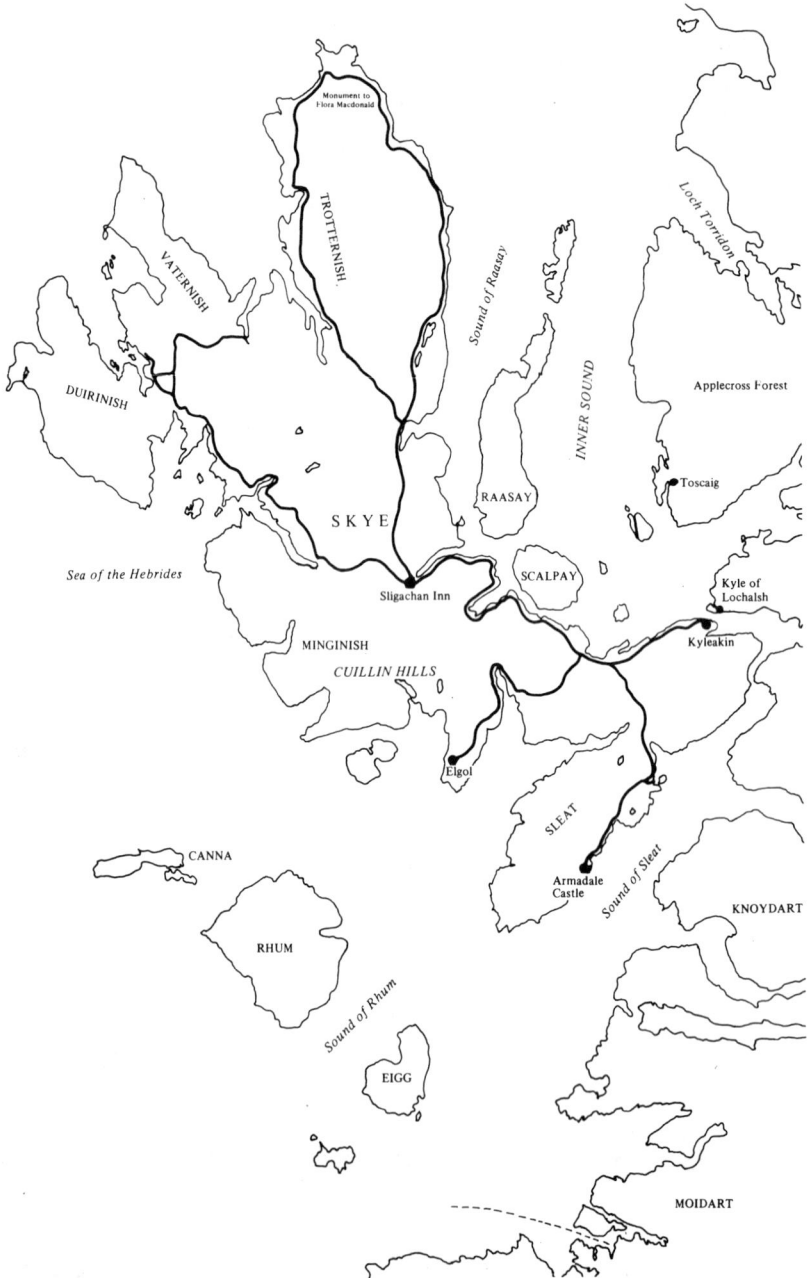